essential
middle eastern
cooking

essential
middle eastern
cooking

AUTHENTIC RECIPES FROM A FASCINATING CUISINE

SOHEILA KIMBERLEY

LORENZ BOOKS

To my husband, for his encouragement and patience —
and for being just William.

This edition published by Lorenz Books
27 West 20th Street, New York, NY 10011

LORENZ BOOKS are available for bulk purchase for sales promotion
and for premium use. For details, write or call the sales director,
Lorenz Books, 27 West 20th Street, New York, NY 10011

© 1996, 2001 Anness Publishing Limited

www.lorenzbooks.com

Lorenz Books is an imprint of Anness Publishing Inc.

A CIP catalogue record for this book is available from the British Library

Publisher: Joanna Lorenz
Senior Cookery Editor: Linda Fraser
Copy Editor: Christine Ingram
Designer: Siân Keogh
Photography and styling: Patrick McLeavey, assisted by Jo Brewer
Food for Photography: Jane Stevenson assisted by Jane Hartshorn
Illustrator: Madeleine David
Pictures on pages 1, 7 and 8: Zefa pictures

Front cover: William Lingwood, Photographer;
Helen Trent, Stylist; Sunil Vijayakar, Food Stylist

Originally published as *Creative Cooking Library: Taste of the Middle East*

1 3 5 7 9 10 8 6 4 2

CONTENTS

INTRODUCTION

For over three thousand years the Middle East has been the crucible of many civilizations – the Babylonians, Armenians, Assyrians, Persians, Greeks and the Romans to name but a few – and in the process it has acquired a rich cosmopolitan character.

While most of us eat to live, the typical Middle Eastern person lives to eat. There is, however, more to it than that – food plays a very important social role. A Persian saying sums up the attitude to food perfectly: *"Mehman Hediyah Khodust"* (A guest is God's gift). And indeed there is no better way to look after a guest than to give him or her good food.

Such is the importance of a guest – whether he or she be a member of your own family, a friend or indeed a stranger – that when food is prepared an extra amount is always added, just on the off chance that someone may stop by during the meal. At our home in Iran, for instance, we always kept open house on Fridays, the equivalent of Sundays in the West, and my mother made sure that plenty of food was prepared in case friends and family paid us a visit, which they invariably did.

This gracious hospitality is typical of the Middle East. The custom can be traced back through centuries, as can the dishes themselves. The Arab word for hors d'oeuvre, for example, is *mezze*, which comes from the Greek *maza* (porridge), a word which embraces taramasalata, hummus and many similar dishes found in both Greek and Middle Eastern cuisines.

While many Middle Eastern dishes have similar origins, every region, every country, every town, and, in days gone by, every family, had their own recipes, their own way of preparing a universal dish. What was known by one name in one country was called something completely different in another. Certain regions have, however, become associated with specific dishes. The Persian *khoresh* is especially interesting, as it can be traced back over two centuries to the time of the Parthians. Their concept of good and evil was reflected in their food. Dishes like *khoreshe hoo*, a blend of lamb with peas and prunes, and *khoreshe ghoureh*, meat with nuts, vinegar and sour grapes, express the Parthian belief in the eternal battle between light and darkness. This balance continues to be the basis of Persian cuisine, although it is doubtful if many cooks are aware of its origins as they prepare *khoresh* in kitchens throughout the world.

Rice is one of the staples of Middle Eastern cuisine, but this was not always the case. The diet originally consisted of millet porridge, coarse bread, olives, figs, beans, cheese and milk. Rice was a luxury, grown on the northern borders of Persia around the Caspian Sea. Gradually it became available to the more wealthy urban dwellers, but it took centuries for rice to become universally adopted. Nowadays we are spoilt with choices of basmati rice and the American long grain varieties, but nothing beats rice from Iran. Its smell, texture and flavor are unique and have to be experienced to be believed. No other Middle Eastern Country prepares rice as the Iranians do; cooking rice to perfection is almost a matter of national pride.

Other important ingredients include milk, honey, yogurt, cheese, fruit and vegetables, especially garlic and onions. Olive oil has long been recognised in the Middle East for its healthy properties. Meat and poultry are valued for their protein content, and if meat is

Freshly picked, ripe cherries are offered for sale from this roadside stall in a bustling Damascus street market near the shores of the Mediterranean.

not used, dried beans, peas and lentils are substituted.

What you will not find in these pages are any recipes which feature pork. The reasons would seem obvious, but the roots are not religious. Had this book been written four millennia ago, pork would have been central to the cuisine, as the pig was a favored animal throughout the region. It was only the invasion of the Indo-Aryan tribes around 2000 BC that signalled its departure. The Indo-Aryans were cattle-rearers. They disliked pigs, which were hard to herd, and which they found offensive due to the dirty conditions the pigs reveled in. It was also very difficult to keep the meat fresh in the heat. The days of the pigs were numbered and they have in fact never returned.

Hot and cold desserts are not common in the Middle East. The main courses tend to be very filling, so fresh fruit is generally preferred at the end of a meal. Sweets are often served on festive occasions, or when entertaining guests for tea.

In the past cooking fats used in the preparation of Middle Eastern dishes tended to be quite heavy. The *alya* or fat from a sheep's or lamb's tail, was particularly popular. Since finding a sheep's or lamb's tail in the local supermarket can be a problem nowadays, I have substituted cooking oil, and in some cases, butter. I've taken similar liberties with other ingredients which I am sure my grandmother would never have countenanced in her dishes, but it's a question of needs must, especially when the ingredients have to be found in Western stores. Through-out the book, however, I've been careful to retain each dish's unique flavor despite minor changes to accommodate the Western palate.

The other aspect I am most aware of is that the dishes must be easy to prepare. Commonsense and creativity have been my watchwords. Naturally

In an Israeli market stall, piled high with dried dates and sweets, a child minds the store.

there is an element of hard work in making some of the dishes, but I have streamlined the processes where possible. I am not afraid of using modern labor-saving devices such as the blender, or using bought ingredients. My grandmother, for example, would have made her own yogurt. I confess that I do not.

As the mother of two teenage daughters and with a husband who is forever hungry, cooking is a necessity, but one which, over the years, has become ever more enjoyable. When I embarked on my culinary journey many years ago on marrying an English husband, meals were a hit-and-miss affair, but he encouraged me to

continue, always praising my cooking and telling me how delicious each dish was. The occasional international telephone call to Tehran to ask my mother how to make a certain dish, or the odd times when everything went wrong are now dim memories, but I would happily go through the learning process again.

With the aid of this book I hope everyone will be able to cook their favorite meals for themselves and experiment with other dishes.

Writing this book and sharing my joy of food with you all has been immensely satisfying and my only regret is that I cannot personally share each and every one of your dishes.

INGREDIENTS

A walk through the bazaar in Tehran provides a wonderful introduction to Middle Eastern ingredients. Shop after shop is packed with aromatics and spices, from rose petals to cinnamon and saffron. You can buy any combination you choose, but the most popular herbs and spices are chives, cinnamon, paprika, saffron and turmeric.

CINNAMON
The powdered form of this spice is widely used in all sorts of Middle Eastern recipes, especially in *khoresh*.

CUMIN
The delicate aroma of the spice is a perfect complement to many vegetable dishes and salads. It is also used in Gulf fish curries. Cumin seeds have a flavor similar to that of caraway. In Middle Eastern cooking cumin is used either whole or ground.

DRIED LIMES
Limu amani are available from Middle Eastern or Greek shops, either whole or crushed, and make a very good alternative to lemon. They are usually cooked with meat and fresh herbs.

EGGPLANT
There are countless ways of preparing this incomparable vegetable, but the secret of preserving the delicate flavor lies in removing any bitterness. This is

Clockwise from top left: garlic, two varieties of eggplant, fava beans (in the shell and loose), baby spinach, vine leaves and red pepper (center).

Dried limes and *zereshk* (on board) with (from left), short grain rice, basmati and long grain rice.

done by slicing or dicing the eggplant into a colander, sprinkling it with salt and allowing it to drain. It is rinsed and dried before use.

FAVA BEANS
Broad beans are available frozen from any supermarket or fresh when in season. Only the tender green center of the bean is used in Middle Eastern cooking, so they need to be shelled if frozen or podded and shelled if fresh. When the fresh beans are cooked with rice and dill for *baghali polo*, they add an exquisite taste and aroma to the dish.

GARLIC
Used extensively throughout the Middle East, garlic is valued for its health properties as well as its flavor.

HERBS
Chives, cilantro, dill, marjoram, mint and parsley are among the most important ingredients in any Middle Eastern kitchen. They are served fresh, traditionally on a separate plate to accompany the food. Fresh herbs are offered with cheese, cooked with meat and rice, mixed into salads and used in stuffings for vegetables. Chopped herbs are used in handfuls, rather than spoonfuls, in all sorts of cooked dishes.

NUTMEG
Whole nutmegs are the hard aromatic seeds of an evergreen tree. The spice is widely used all over the world. Whole nutmegs can be grated for cooking, but in Middle Eastern dishes it is most usual to use the ground spice.

A selection of nuts, clockwise from top left: (on board) pine nuts, hazelnuts and almonds; walnuts and pistachio nuts.

NUTS

Nuts are widely used in Middle Eastern cooking and are often combined with rice, but how they are used depends on the country. In Iran, for instance, walnuts are ground, cooked with either chicken or duck and made into a delicious sauce with pomegranate juice or sour cherries. Almonds, hazelnuts, pistachios and pine nuts are not only combined with rice and used in savory stuffings, but are also used to fill sweets such as baklava.

PAPRIKA

Although paprika is often associated with Eastern Europe it is widely used in the Middle East in soups, meat dishes, salad dressings and garnishes.

RED BELL PEPPERS

Widely used, red bell peppers make a delicious meal when stuffed or cooked with meat and eggplants. When grilled, they acquire a smoky flavor, and are a tasty salad ingredient.

RICE

Rice is the most common ingredient in Middle Eastern cooking. Basmati rice has an exquisite taste and aroma. Long grain American rice gives adequate results, while short grain rice is mainly used for desserts.

SAFFRON

Derived from the dried stamens of a type of crocus, saffron has a superb aroma and flavor. It also adds a delicate color to food. For the best results the saffron should be ground to a powder and diluted in a small amount of boiling water.

SPINACH

Fresh baby spinach leaves are available from grocers and supermarkets throughout the year. In the Midde East, spinach is often cooked with meat or combined with yogurt to make a popular vegetarian appetizer.

SUMAC

These edible red berries are dried and crushed to a powder and are delicious sprinkled on kebabs, fish dishes and all sorts of salads.

TURMERIC

This spice originated in Iran. It adds a distinctive flavor and rich yellow color to meat and rice dishes. It is very widely used throughout the Middle East and India.

A selection of spices, left to right from top row: ground *sumac*, saffron threads, paprika, cinnamon sticks, turmeric, cardamom pods, ground nutmeg, whole nutmegs and cumin seeds.

VINE LEAVES

When stuffed with meat, lentils and herbs, these make delicious appetizers.

ZERESHK

This is a small sour berry that grows on trees by the water in the warmer part of Iran. It is traditionally served with Persian rice dishes.

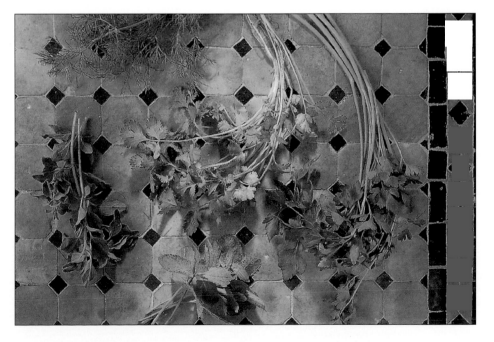

A selection of fresh herbs, clockwise from top left: dill, flat leaf parsley, mint, marjoram and cilantro (center).

SOUPS AND APPETIZERS

It is for mezze *— the marvelous array of hot and cold dishes served as appetizers — that the Middle East is particularly well known. A special meal may commence with a selection of twenty or more, from a simple spinach and yogurt salad to wedges of a complex herb and vegetable egg pie. Taramasalata, Hummus, and Eggplant and Tahini Dip are delicious when scooped up with pita bread, while tiny pastries, stuffed vegetables and salads complete the spread. In addition to chilled yogurt-based soups, the chapter includes some winter warmers.*

Beef and Herb Soup with Yogurt

This classic Iranian soup, *Aashe Maste*, is almost a meal in itself. It is full of invigorating herbs, and is a popular cold weather dish.

INGREDIENTS

Serves 6

2 large onions
2 tablespoons oil
1 tablespoon ground turmeric
½ cup yellow split peas
5 cups water
8 ounces ground beef
1 cup rice
3 tablespoons each fresh chopped
    parsley, cilantro and chives
1 tablespoon butter
1 large garlic clove, finely chopped
4 tablespoons chopped mint
2–3 saffron strands dissolved in
    1 tablespoon boiling water (optional)
salt and freshly ground black pepper
yogurt and nan bread, to serve

1 Chop one of the onions, then heat the oil in a large saucepan and fry the onion until golden brown. Add the turmeric, split peas and water, bring to a boil, then reduce the heat and simmer for 20 minutes.

—— COOK'S TIP ——

Fresh spinach is also delicious in this soup. Add 2 ounces finely chopped spinach leaves to the soup with the parsley, cilantro and chives.

2 Grate the other onion into a bowl, add the ground beef and seasoning and mix well. Using your hands, form the mixture into small balls, about the size of walnuts. Carefully add to the pan and simmer for 10 minutes.

3 Add the rice, then stir in the parsley, cilantro, and chives and simmer for about 30 minutes, until the rice is tender, stirring frequently.

4 Melt the butter in a small pan and gently fry the garlic. Add the mint, stir briefly and sprinkle over the soup with the saffron, if using.

5 Spoon the soup into warmed serving dishes and serve with yogurt and nan bread.

Spinach and Lemon Soup with Meatballs

Aarshe Saak is almost standard fare in many parts of the Middle East. In Greece it is made with rice and chicken stock only and called Avgolemono.

INGREDIENTS

Serves 6
2 large onions
3 tablespoons oil
1 tablespoon ground turmeric
½ cup yellow split peas
5 cups water
8 ounces ground lamb
1 pound spinach, chopped
½ cup rice flour or cornstarch
juice of 2 lemons
1–2 garlic cloves, very
   finely chopped
2 tablespoons chopped fresh mint
4 eggs, beaten
salt and freshly ground black pepper

1 Chop one of the onions, heat 2 tablespoons of the oil in a large frying pan and fry the onion until golden. Add the turmeric, split peas and water and bring to a boil. Reduce the heat to medium and simmer for about 20 minutes.

2 Grate the other onion. Put it into a bowl, add the ground lamb and seasoning and mix well. Using your hands, form the mixture into small balls, about the size of walnuts. Carefully add to the pan and simmer for 10 minutes, then add the chopped spinach, cover and simmer for 20 minutes.

3 Mix the rice flour or cornstarch with about 1 cup cold water to make a smooth paste, then slowly add to the pan, stirring all the time to prevent lumps. Stir in the lemon juice, season with salt and pepper and cook over a gentle heat for 20 minutes.

4 Meanwhile, heat the remaining oil in a small pan and fry the garlic briefly until golden. Stir in the mint and remove the pan from the heat.

5 Remove the soup from the heat and stir in the beaten eggs. Sprinkle the garlic and mint garnish over the soup and serve.

COOK'S TIP

If preferred, use less lemon juice to begin with and then add more to taste once the soup is cooked.

Spinach and Yogurt Borani

This popular appetizer from Iran, called *Borani Esfanaj*, is as simple as it is healthy.

INGREDIENTS

Serves 4
2 tablespoons butter or margarine
1 large onion, chopped
2 garlic cloves, crushed
1 pound fresh spinach, chopped
2 cups plain yogurt
salt and freshly ground black pepper

—— COOK'S TIP ——

Use 8 ounces thawed, frozen spinach if fresh spinach is not available.

1 Melt the butter or margarine in a large saucepan and fry the onion until golden brown. Add the garlic and chopped spinach and continue frying, stirring occasionally. The spinach will cook in its own moisture. Continue cooking over a low heat until all the moisture has evaporated.

2 Stir the yogurt into the spinach mixture. Season with salt and pepper, mix well and then allow to cool completely before serving.

Lentil Soup

This traditional Turkish soup makes an ideal winter lunch.

INGREDIENTS

Serves 4
3 tablespoons olive oil
1 large onion, chopped
1 celery stalk, chopped
2½ cups red lentils
5 cups meat stock
4–5 tomatoes
juice of 1 lemon
½ teaspoon chili powder (optional)
salt and freshly ground black pepper

1 Heat the oil in a large saucepan and cook the onion and celery over a gentle heat until soft. Add the lentils and stock to the pan, bring to a boil and then simmer for 25 minutes until the lentils are soft.

2 Peel the tomatoes byfirst dipping them into boiling water for about 30 seconds to loosen the skins.

3 Chop the tomatoes coarsely on a chopping board with a sharp knife, and add to the pan with the lemon juice, salt and pepper and the chili powder, if using. Simmer for another 10 minutes and serve.

—— COOK'S TIP ——

Yellow and/or brown lentils can be used instead of red lentils, if preferred. They may take slightly longer to cook.

Dolmeh

Dolmeh, meaning "stuffed" in Persian, generally refers to any vegetable or fruit stuffed with meat, rice and herbs. It is a favorite dish throughout the Middle East.

INGREDIENTS

Serves 4–6
9 ounces vine leaves
2 tablespoons olive oil
1 large onion, finely chopped
9 ounces ground lamb
¼ cup yellow split peas
½ cup cooked rice
2 tablespoons chopped fresh parsley
2 tablespoons chopped fresh mint
2 tablespoons chopped fresh chives
3–4 scallions, finely chopped
juice of 2 lemons
2 tablespoons tomato paste (optional)
2 tablespoons sugar
salt and freshly ground black pepper
yogurt and pita bread, to serve

1 Blanch fresh vine leaves, if using, in boiling water for 1–2 minutes to soften them, or rinse preserved bottled or canned vine leaves under cold water.

2 Heat the olive oil in a large frying pan and fry the onion for a few minutes until slightly softened. Add the meat and fry over a moderate heat until well browned, stirring frequently. Season with salt and pepper.

3 Place the split peas in a small pan with enough water to cover and bring to a boil. Cover the pan and simmer gently over a low heat for 12–15 minutes until soft. Drain the split peas if necessary.

4 Stir the split peas, cooked rice, chopped herbs, scallions, and the juice of one of the lemons into the meat. Add the tomato paste, if using, and then knead the mixture with your hands until thoroughly blended.

5 Place a vine leaf on a chopping board with the vein side up. Place 1 tablespoon of the meat mixture on the vine leaf and fold the stem end over the meat. Fold the sides in towards the center and then fold over to make a neat package. Continue until all the filling has been used up.

6 Line the bottom of a large saucepan with several unstuffed leaves and arrange the rolled leaves in tight layers on top. Stir the remaining lemon juice and the sugar into about ⅔ cup water and pour over the leaves. Place a small heat-resistant plate over the *dolmeh* to keep them in shape. Cover the pan with a tightly fitting lid and cook over a very low heat for 2 hours, checking occasionally and adding a little extra water if the pan begins to boil dry. Serve warm or cold with yogurt and warm pita bread.

COOK'S TIP

If using preserved vine leaves, soak them overnight in cold water and then, if you have time, rinse several times before use.

Stuffed Bell Peppers

Stuffed peppers or *Dolmeh Felfel* make a tasty and attractive appetizer, especially when all four colors of pepper are used.

INGREDIENTS

Serves 6

6 bell peppers (red, yellow and green)
2 tablespoons olive oil
1 large onion, finely chopped
3–4 scallions, finely chopped
9 ounces ground lamb
2 garlic cloves, crushed (optional)
¼ cup yellow split peas
½ cup cooked rice
2 tablespoons chopped fresh parsley
2 tablespoons finely chopped
   fresh mint
2 tablespoons chopped fresh chives
1 teaspoon ground cinnamon
juice of 2 lemons
2 tablespoons tomato paste (optional)
14-ounce can chopped tomatoes
pat of butter
salt and freshly ground black pepper
yogurt and pita bread or nan, to serve

1 Cut off the mixed pepper tops and set aside. Remove the seeds and cores and trim the bases so they stand squarely. Cook in boiling salted water for 5 minutes, then drain, rinse under cold water and set aside.

2 Heat the oil in a large saucepan or flameproof casserole and fry the onion and scallions for about 4–5 minutes until golden brown. Add the meat and fry over a moderate heat until well browned, stirring frequently. Stir in the garlic if using.

3 Place the split peas in a small pan with enough water to cover, bring to a boil and then simmer gently for 12–15 minutes until soft. Drain.

4 Stir the split peas, cooked rice, herbs, cinnamon, juice of one of the lemons, and the tomato paste, if using, into the meat. Season with salt and pepper and stir again until all are well combined.

5 Spoon the rice and split pea mixture into the peppers and place the reserved lids on top.

6 Pour the chopped tomatoes into a large saucepan or flameproof casserole and add the remaining lemon juice and the butter. Arrange the peppers neatly in the pan with the stems upwards. Bring to a boil and then cover tightly and cook over a low heat for 40–45 minutes until the peppers are tender.

7 Serve the peppers with the tomato sauce accompanied by yogurt and warm pita bread or nan.

─── COOK'S TIP ───

Make sure that the saucepan or casserole that you choose is just large enough so that the peppers fit quite snugly.

Fattoush

This simple peasant salad has become a popular dish all over Syria and the Lebanon.

INGREDIENTS

Serves 4

1 yellow or red bell pepper
1 large cucumber
4–5 tomatoes
1 bunch scallions
2 tablespoons finely chopped
    fresh parsley
2 tablespoons finely chopped fresh mint
2 tablespoons finely chopped
    fresh cilantro
2 garlic cloves, crushed
5 tablespoons olive oil
juice of 2 lemons
salt and freshly ground black pepper
2 pita breads

1 Slice the pepper, discarding the seeds and core, then coarsely chop the cucumber and tomatoes. Place them in a large salad bowl.

2 Trim and slice the scallions. Add to the cucumber, tomatoes and pepper with the finely chopped parsley, mint and cilantro.

3 To make the dressing, blend the garlic with the olive oil and lemon juice in a cup, then season to taste with salt and black pepper. Pour the dressing over the salad and toss lightly to mix.

4 Toast the pita bread in a toaster or under a hot broiler until crisp and then serve it with the salad.

----- VARIATION -----

If you prefer, make this salad in the traditional way. After toasting the pita bread until crisp, crush it in your hand and then sprinkle it over the salad before serving.

----- COOK'S TIP -----

Although the recipe calls for only 2 tablespoons of each of the herbs, if you have plenty to hand, then you can add as much as you like to this aromatic salad.

Baked Eggs with Herbs and Vegetables

Eggs, baked or fried as omelets with vegetables and herbs and sometimes meat, too, are popular throughout the Middle East. This particular dish, *Kuku Sabzi*, comes from Persia and is a traditional New Year favorite.

INGREDIENTS

Serves 4–6

2–3 saffron strands
8 eggs
2 leeks
4 ounces fresh spinach
½ iceberg lettuce
4 scallions
3 tablespoons chopped fresh parsley
3 tablespoons chopped fresh chives
3 tablespoons chopped fresh cilantro
1 garlic clove, crushed
2 tablespoons chopped walnuts
  (optional)
2 tablespoons butter
salt and freshly ground black pepper
yogurt and pita bread, to serve

1 Preheat the oven to 350°F. Soak the saffron strands in 1 tablespoon boiling water.

COOK'S TIP

To bring out their flavor, lightly toast the walnuts in a moderate oven, or under a hot broiler before chopping.

2 Beat the eggs in a large bowl. Chop the leeks, spinach, lettuce and scallions finely and add to the eggs together with the chopped herbs, garlic, and walnuts, if using. Season with salt and pepper, add the saffron water and stir thoroughly to mix.

3 Melt the butter in a large shallow casserole and pour in the vegetable and egg mixture.

4 Bake in the oven for 35–40 minutes until the egg mixture is set and the top is golden. Serve hot or cold, cut into wedges, with yogurt and pita bread.

Böreks

In Turkey, little stuffed pastries are very popular. They are easy to make and are ideal for parties or as finger canapés.

INGREDIENTS

Makes 35–40
8 ounces feta cheese, grated
8 ounces mozzarella, grated
2 eggs, beaten
3 tablespoons chopped fresh parsley
3 tablespoons chopped fresh chives
3 tablespoons chopped fresh mint
pinch of nutmeg
8 ounces filo pastry
3–4 tablespoon melted butter
freshly ground black pepper

1 Preheat the oven to 350°F. In a bowl, blend the feta and mozzarella cheeses with the beaten eggs. Add the chopped parsley, chives and mint, and season with black pepper and nutmeg. Stir well to mix.

2 Cut the sheets of pastry into four rectangular strips about 3 inches wide. Cover all but one or two strips of the pastry with a damp cloth to prevent them from drying out.

3 Brush one strip of pastry at a time with a little melted butter.

4 Place 1 teaspoon of filling at the bottom edge. Fold one corner over the filling to make a triangle shape. Continue folding the pastry over itself until you get to the end of the strip. Keep making triangles until all the mixture is used up.

5 Place the *böreks* on a greased baking tray and bake in the oven for about 30 minutes until golden brown and crisp. Serve warm or cold.

COOK'S TIP

A mixture of almost any cheeses can be used but avoid cream cheeses.

Eggplant and Tahini Dip

Baba ghanouj is a Turkish variation of a Middle Eastern dish. It is said to have been invented by the ladies of the sultan's harem – to win his favor.

INGREDIENTS

Serves 4–6
3 eggplants
2 garlic cloves, crushed
4 tablespoons tahini
juice of 2 lemons
1 tablespoon paprika
salt and freshly ground black pepper
chopped fresh parsley, olive oil plus a
   few olives, to garnish
    pita bread or crudités, to serve

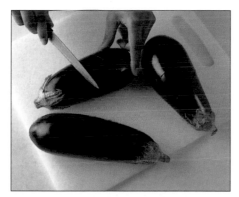

1 Preheat the oven to 375°F. Slit the skins of the eggplants, place them on a baking sheet and bake in the oven for 30–40 minutes until the skins begin to split.

2 Place the eggplants on a chopping board. Carefully peel away the skins from the eggplants.

3 Place the eggplant flesh in a blender or food processor. Add the garlic, tahini, lemon juice, paprika and salt and pepper. Blend to a smooth paste, adding about 1–2 tablespoons water if the paste is too thick.

4 Spoon into a dish and make a dip in the center. Garnish with paprika, chopped parsley, a drizzle of olive oil and olives. Serve with hot pita bread or a selection of crudités.

—————— COOK'S TIP ——————

Tahini can be obtained from health food stores and good supermarkets.

Eggplant with Tomatoes and Eggs

Mirza Ghasemi is a specialty of northern Iran. Serve it with warm pita bread for an unusual lunch or as an appetizer.

Ingredients

Serves 4–6

4 eggplants
½ cup butter or margarine
1 large onion, finely chopped
2 garlic cloves, crushed
4 large tomatoes, peeled, seeded and
   chopped
4 eggs
salt and freshly ground black pepper

─────── Cook's Tip ───────

Peel the tomatoes by first dipping them in boiling water to loosen the skins.

1 Preheat the oven to 375°F. Carefully slit the skins of the eggplants, place them on a baking sheet and bake in the oven for 30–40 minutes until the skins begin to split.

2 Meanwhile, melt 4 tablespoons of the butter or margarine in a large frying pan and fry the onion and garlic over medium heat for 4–5 minutes until softened. Add the tomatoes and fry for another 2–3 minutes.

3 Peel the eggplants, finely chop the flesh and stir into the pan with the onion and tomatoes. Cook for about 4–5 minutes, stirring frequently.

4 Melt the remaining butter or margarine in a small frying pan, add the beaten eggs and cook over a low heat until the eggs are just beginning to set, stirring occasionally with a fork. Stir the eggs into the eggplant mixture, season to taste and serve.

Taramasalata

This delicious Turkish and Greek specialty makes an excellent appetizer.

Ingredients

Serves 4

4 ounces tarama
2 garlic cloves, crushed
2 tablespoons grated onion
4 tablespoons olive oil
4 slices white bread, crusts removed
juice of 2 lemons
2 tablespoons water or milk
paprika, to garnish (optional)

─────── Cook's Tip ───────

Tarama is usually salted carp roe. It is sold in 10-ounce jars in the refrigerated sections of Greek and Middle Eastern delicatessens and some supermarkets.

1 Place the tarama, garlic, onion, olive oil, bread and lemon juice in a blender or food processor and process until smooth.

2 Add the water or milk and process again for a few seconds. (This will give the taramasalata a creamier taste.)

3 Pour the taramasalata into a serving bowl, cover with plastic wrap and chill for 1–2 hours before serving. Just before serving, sprinkle with a little paprika, if desired.

Falafel

These tasty patties are one of the national dishes of Egypt. They can also be made with dried fava beans or chick-peas, and make an excellent appetizer.

INGREDIENTS

Serves 6

2½ cups dried white beans
2 red onions, chopped
2 large garlic cloves, crushed
3 tablespoons finely chopped
   fresh parsley
1 teaspoon ground coriander
1 teaspoon ground cumin
1½ teaspoons baking powder
oil, for deep frying
salt and freshly ground black pepper
tomato salad, to serve

1 Soak the white beans overnight in water. Remove the skins and process in a blender or food processor. Add the chopped onions, garlic, parsley, coriander, cumin, baking powder and seasoning and blend again to make a very smooth paste. Allow the mixture to stand at room temperature for at least 30 minutes.

2 Take walnut-sized pieces of mixture and flatten into small patties. Set aside again for about 15 minutes.

3 Heat the oil until it's very hot and then fry the patties in batches until golden brown. Drain on kitchen paper and then serve with a tomato salad.

Hummus

This popular Middle Eastern dip is widely available in supermarkets, but nothing compares with the delicious home-made variety.

INGREDIENTS

Serves 4–6

1 cup cooked chick-peas
½ cup tahini
3 garlic cloves
juice of 2 lemons
3–4 tablespoons water
salt and freshly ground black pepper
fresh radishes, to serve

For the garnish

1 tablespoon olive oil
1 tablespoon finely chopped
   fresh parsley
½ teaspoon paprika
4 black olives

1 Place the chick-peas, tahini, garlic, lemon juice, seasoning and a little of the water in a blender or food processor. Process until smooth, adding a little more water, if necessary.

2 Alternatively, if you don't have a blender or food processor, mix the ingredients together in a small bowl until smooth.

3 Spoon the mixture into a shallow dish. Make a dent in the middle and pour the olive oil into it. Garnish with parsley, paprika and olives and serve with the radishes.

COOK'S TIP

Canned chick-peas can be used for hummus. Drain and rinse under cold water before processing.

MEAT DISHES

Lamb and beef feature strongly on Middle Eastern menus. This chapter includes well-known dishes like kebabs, couscous and koftas, but also introduces the delicious range of stews known in Iran as khoresh, *which combine various types of meat or poultry with fruits, herbs and spices. Long, slow cooking allows the flavors to blend to produce a delicious mellow result. Stewing and grilling are the most popular cooking methods, but when meat is roasted or sautéed, it is often marinated in yogurt for tenderness and extra flavor.*

Tangy Beef and Herb Khoresh

Lamb, beef or poultry stews combined with vegetables, fruit, herbs and spices, are called *khoresh* in Farsi and are among the most loved of Persian dishes. Like this beef stew, *Khoreshe Gormeh Sabzi*, they are mildly spiced and are ideal for a simple but delicious dinner party.

INGREDIENTS

Serves 4
3 tablespoons oil
1 large onion, chopped
1 pound lean stewing beef, cubed
1 tablespoon chopped fenugreek leaf
2 teaspoons ground turmeric
½ teaspoon ground cinnamon
2½ cups water
1 ounce fresh parsley, chopped
1 ounce fresh chives, chopped
15-ounce can red kidney beans
juice of 1 lemon
salt and freshly ground black pepper
rice, to serve

1 Heat 2 tablespoons of the oil in a large saucepan or flameproof casserole and fry the onion for about 3–4 minutes until light golden. Add the beef and fry for another 5–10 minutes until browned, stirring so that the meat browns on all sides.

2 Add the fenugreek, turmeric and cinnamon and cook for about 1 minute, stirring, then add the water and bring to a boil. Cover and simmer over a low heat for 45 minutes, stirring occasionally.

3 Heat the remaining oil in a small frying pan and fry the parsley and chives over a moderate heat for 2–3 minutes, stirring frequently.

4 Drain the kidney beans and stir them into the beef with the herbs and lemon juice. Season with salt and pepper. Simmer the stew for another 30–35 minutes, until the meat is tender. Serve on a bed of rice.

Lamb with Split Peas

Khoreshe Ghaimeh is another traditional Persian dish and is always served at parties and religious ceremonies. It is a great favorite with children too!

INGREDIENTS

Serves 4

2 tablespoons butter or margarine
1 large onion, chopped
1 pound lean lamb, cut into
 small cubes
1 teaspoon ground turmeric
1 teaspoon ground cinnamon
1 teaspoon curry powder
1¼ cups water
2–3 saffron strands
½ cup yellow split peas
3 *limu amani* (dried limes)
3–4 tomatoes, chopped
2 tablespoons oil
2 large potatoes, chopped
salt and freshly ground black pepper
rice, to serve

1 Melt the butter or margarine in a large saucepan or flameproof casserole and fry the onion for 3–4 minutes until golden, stirring occasionally. Add the meat and cook over a high heat for another 3–4 minutes until it has browned.

2 Add the turmeric, cinnamon and curry powder and cook for about 2 minutes, stirring frequently.

3 Stir in the water, season well and bring to a boil, then cover and simmer over a low heat for about 30–35 minutes, until the meat is half cooked. Stir the saffron into about 1 tablespoon boiling water.

4 Add the saffron to the meat with the split peas, *limu amani* and tomatoes. Stir well and then simmer, covered, for another 35 minutes until the meat is completely tender.

5 Heat the oil in a frying pan and fry the potatoes for about 10–15 minutes, until cooked and golden. Lift out the *limu amani* and discard. Spoon the meat onto a large serving dish and scatter the potatoes on top. Serve the *khoresh* with rice.

COOK'S TIP

Limu amani (dried limes) are available in all Persian or Middle Eastern stores. However, if you have difficulty obtaining them, use the juice of either 2 limes or 1 lemon instead. If you prefer, you can use lean stewing beef in place of the lamb in this traditional *khoresh*.

Lamb and Celery Khoresh

This unusual stew, *Khoreshe Karafs*, has a lovely fresh taste.

INGREDIENTS

Serves 4
1 large onion, chopped
3 tablespoons butter
1 pound lean lamb, cubed
1 teaspoon ground turmeric
½ teaspoon ground cinnamon
2½ cups water
1 head of celery, chopped
¼ cup fresh parsley, chopped
1 small bunch of fresh mint, chopped
juice of 1 lemon
salt and freshly ground black pepper
mint leaves, to garnish
rice, and cucumber and tomato
   salad, to serve

1 Fry the onion in 2 tablespoons of the butter in a large saucepan or flameproof casserole for 3–4 minutes.

2 Add the meat and cook for 2–3 minutes until browned, stirring frequently, then stir in the turmeric, cinnamon and salt and pepper.

3 Add the water and bring to a boil, then reduce the heat, cover and simmer for about 30 minutes until the meat is half cooked.

4 Melt the remaining butter in a frying pan and fry the celery for 8–10 minutes, until tender, stirring frequently. Add the parsley and mint and fry for another 3–4 minutes.

5 Stir the celery and herbs together with the lemon juice into the meat and simmer, covered, for another 25–30 minutes until the meat is completely tender. Serve garnished with mint leaves and accompanied by rice and a cucumber and tomato salad.

COOK'S TIP

If you prefer, this dish can be made with canned or chopped fresh tomatoes in place of some of the herbs. Add the tomatoes in step 4 at the same time as the celery.

Lamb with Spinach and Prunes

If you like fresh spinach you will love this delicious, lightly spiced, sweet and sour dish known as *Khoreshe Esanaj*.

INGREDIENTS

Serves 4
3 tablespoons oil
1 large onion, chopped
1 pound lean lamb, cubed
½ teaspoon grated nutmeg
1 teaspoon ground cinnamon
2½ cups water
1¼ cups chives or scallions, including
   green parts, finely chopped
1 pound fresh spinach, chopped
1¾ cups prunes, soaked
juice of 1 lemon
salt and freshly ground black pepper
rice, to serve

1 Heat 2 tablespoons of the oil and fry the onion for 3–4 minutes until golden. Add the lamb and fry until brown on all sides, then sprinkle over the nutmeg and cinnamon and stir well.

2 Add the water, bring to a boil and spoon off any scum that rises to the surface. Season with salt and pepper and then cover and simmer over a low heat for 40–45 minutes until the meat is nearly cooked.

3 Heat the remaining oil in another large pan, add the chives or scallions, stir-fry for a few minutes and then add the spinach. Cover and cook over a moderate heat for 2–3 minutes until the spinach has wilted and then add this mixture to the meat, with the prunes and lemon juice.

4 Cook, covered, for another 20–25 minutes, until the meat is completely tender. Serve with rice.

Ground Meat Kebabs

In the Middle East, these kebabs are known as *Kabab Kobideh* and are often served with rice into which is stirred raw egg yolk and melted butter. Traditionally, they are barbecued, but can also be cooked under a hot broiler.

INGREDIENTS

Serves 6–8
1 pound lean lamb
1 pound lean beef
1 large onion, grated
2 garlic cloves, crushed
1 tablespoon *sumac* (optional)
2 teaspoons baking soda
2–3 saffron strands, soaked in
   1 tablespoon boiling water
6–8 tomatoes, halved
1 tablespoon melted butter
salt and freshly ground black pepper

1 Grind the lamb and beef two or three times until very finely ground, place in a large bowl and add the grated onion, garlic, *sumac*, if using, soaked saffron, baking soda and salt and pepper.

2 Knead by hand for several minutes until the mixture is very glutinous. It helps to have a bowl of water nearby in which to dip your fingers to keep the meat from sticking to them.

3 Take a small handful of meat and roll it into a ball. If the ball seems crumbly, knead the mixture in the bowl for a few more minutes.

4 Shape the ball around a flat skewer, molding it around the skewer. Repeat with three or four more balls on each skewer, pressing them tightly to prevent the meat from

5 Thread the tomatoes onto separate skewers and prepare a barbecue grill. When the coals are ready, grill the meat and tomato kebabs for about 10 minutes, basting them with the melted butter and turning occasionally.

COOK'S TIP

Sumac is a favourite Lebanese spice with a slightly sour but fruity flavor. It is available in most Middle Eastern food stores, but it is not essential in this recipe.

Sautéed Lamb with Yogurt

In the Middle East meat is normally stewed or barbecued. Here's a delicious exception from Turkey where the lamb is pan-fried instead.

INGREDIENTS

Serves 4

1 pound lean lamb, preferably boned leg, cubed
3 tablespoons butter
4 tomatoes, skinned and chopped
4 thick slices of bread, crusts removed
1 cup strained plain yogurt
2 garlic cloves, crushed
salt and freshly ground black pepper
paprika and mint leaves, to garnish

For the marinade
½ cup strained plain yogurt
1 large onion, grated

1 First make the marinade: blend together the yogurt, onion and a little seasoning in a large bowl. Add the cubed lamb, cover loosely with plastic wrap and set aside to marinate in a cool place for at least 1 hour.

2 Melt half the butter in a frying pan and fry the meat for 5–10 minutes, until tender but still moist. Transfer to a plate with a slotted spoon and keep warm while cooking the tomatoes.

3 Melt the remaining butter in the same pan and fry the tomatoes for 4–5 minutes until soft. Meanwhile, toast the bread and arrange in the bottom of a shallow serving dish.

4 Season the tomatoes and then spread over the toasted bread in an even layer.

5 Blend the yogurt and garlic and season with salt and pepper. Spoon over the tomatoes.

6 Arrange the meat in a layer on top. Sprinkle with paprika and mint leaves and serve at once.

Persian Kebabs

Kebabs are eaten throughout the Middle East and almost always cooked over a wood or charcoal fire. There are many variations; this particular recipe, *Kabab Bahrg*, comes from Iran and many restaurants serve only this dish.

INGREDIENTS

Serves 4
1 pound lean lamb or beef fillet
2–3 saffron strands
1 large onion, grated
4–6 tomatoes, halved
1 tablespoon butter, melted
salt and freshly ground black pepper
3 tablespoons *sumac*, to garnish
(optional)
rice, to serve

1 Place the meat on a chopping board. Using a sharp knife remove any excess fat from the meat and cut the meat into strips, about ½ inch thick and 1½ inches long.

2 Soak the saffron in 1 tablespoon boiling water, pour into a small bowl and mix with the grated onion. Add to the meat and stir a few times so that the meat is coated thoroughly. Cover loosely with plastic wrap and let marinate overnight in the fridge.

3 Season the meat with salt and pepper and then thread onto flat skewers, aligning the strips in neat rows. Thread the tomatoes onto two separate skewers.

4 Grill the kebabs and tomatoes over hot charcoal for 10–12 minutes, basting with butter and turning occasionally. Serve with rice, sprinkled with *sumac*, if you like.

Shish Kebab

INGREDIENTS

Serves 4
1 pound boned leg of lamb, cubed
1 large green bell pepper, seeded and
  cut into squares
1 large yellow bell pepper, seeded and
  cut into squares
8 baby onions, halved
8 ounces button mushrooms
4 tomatoes, halved
1 tablespoon melted butter
bulgur wheat, to serve

For the marinade

3 tablespoons olive oil
juice of 1 lemon
2 garlic cloves, crushed
1 large onion, grated
1 tablespoon fresh oregano
salt and freshly ground black pepper

1 First make the marinade: blend together the oil, lemon juice, garlic, onion, oregano and seasoning. Place the meat in a shallow dish and pour over the marinade.

2 Cover with plastic wrap and let marinate overnight in the fridge.

3 Thread the cubes of lamb on to skewers, alternating with pieces of green and yellow pepper, onions and mushrooms. Thread the tomatoes on to separate skewers. Grill the kebabs and tomatoes over hot charcoal for 10–12 minutes, basting with butter. Serve with bulgur wheat.

Lebanese Kibbeh

The national dish of Syria and the Lebanon is *kibbeh*, a kind of meatball made from ground lamb and bulgur wheat. Raw *kibbeh* is the most widely eaten type, but this version is very popular too.

INGREDIENTS

Serves 6

¾ cup bulgur wheat
1 pound finely ground lean lamb
1 large onion, grated
1 tablespoon melted butter
salt and freshly ground black pepper
sprigs of mint, to garnish
rice, to serve

For the filling

2 tablespoons oil
1 onion, finely chopped
8 ounces ground lamb or veal
½ cup pine nuts
½ teaspoon ground allspice

For the yogurt dip

2½ cups strained plain yogurt
2–3 garlic cloves, crushed
1–2 tablespoons chopped fresh mint

1 Preheat the oven to 375°F. Rinse the bulgur wheat in a sieve and squeeze out the excess moisture.

2 Mix the lamb, onion and seasoning, kneading the mixture to make a thick paste. Add the bulgur wheat and blend together.

3 To make the filling, heat the oil in a frying pan and fry the onion until golden. Add the lamb or veal and cook, stirring, until evenly browned and then add the pine nuts, allspice and salt and pepper.

4 Oil a large baking pan and spread half of the meat and bulgur wheat mixture over the bottom. Spoon over the filling and top with a second layer of meat and bulgur wheat, pressing down firmly with the back of a spoon.

5 Pour the melted butter over the top and then bake in the oven for 40–45 minutes until browned on top.

6 Meanwhile make the yogurt dip: blend together the yogurt and garlic, spoon into a serving bowl and sprinkle with the chopped mint.

7 Cut the cooked *kibbeh* into squares or rectangles and serve garnished with mint and accompanied by rice and the yogurt dip.

Koftas in Tomato Sauce

There are many varieties of *kofta* in the Middle East. This is a popular version from Turkey.

INGREDIENTS

Serves 4

12 ounces ground lamb or beef
½ cup fresh bread crumbs
1 onion, grated
3 tablespoons chopped fresh parsley
1 tablespoon chopped fresh mint
1 teaspoon ground cumin
1 teaspoon ground turmeric
3 tablespoons oil for frying
salt and freshly ground black pepper
egg noodles, to serve
mint leaves, to garnish

For the tomato sauce

1 tablespoon oil
1 onion, chopped
14-ounce can plum tomatoes
1 tablespoon tomato paste
juice of ½ lemon
salt and freshly ground black pepper

— COOK'S TIP —

Instead of using either ground lamb or beef, use a mixture of the two, if you like.

1 First make the tomato sauce: heat the oil in a large saucepan or flameproof casserole and fry the onion until golden. Stir in the canned tomatoes, tomato paste, lemon juice and seasoning, bring to a boil and then reduce the heat and simmer for about 10 minutes.

2 Meanwhile, place the ground lamb or beef in a large bowl and mix in the bread crumbs, grated onion, herbs and spices and a little salt and pepper.

3 Knead the mixture by hand until thoroughly blended and then shape the mixture into walnut-size balls and place on a plate.

4 Heat the oil in a frying pan and fry the meatballs, in batches if necessary, until evenly browned. Transfer them into the tomato sauce. Cover the pan and simmer very gently for about 30 minutes. Serve with noodles and garnish with mint leaves.

Spiced Roast Lamb

This is a very tasty Turkish version of a roast dinner.

INGREDIENTS

Serves 6–8
6-pound leg of lamb
3–4 large garlic cloves, halved
4 tablespoons olive oil
2 teaspoons paprika
2 teaspoons Dijon mustard
juice of 1 lemon
½ teaspoon dried thyme
½ teaspoon dried rosemary
½ teaspoon sugar
½ cup white wine
salt and freshly ground black pepper
fresh thyme, to garnish
rice and green salad, to serve

COOK'S TIP

This dish is equally delicious served with roast potatoes and vegetables. Let the meat rest for 15 minutes, before slicing.

1 Trim the fat from the lamb and make several incisions in the meat with a sharp knife. Press the garlic halves into the slits.

2 Blend together the olive oil, paprika, mustard, lemon juice, herbs, sugar and seasoning and rub this paste all over the meat. Place the leg of lamb in a shallow dish and allow to stand in a cool place for 1–2 hours.

3 Preheat the oven to 400°F. Place the lamb in a roasting pan, add the wine and cook for 20 minutes. Reduce the heat to 325°F and cook for another 2 hours, basting occasionally. Serve the lamb garnished with thyme and accompanied by rice and a salad.

Roast Leg of Lamb with Saffron

INGREDIENTS

Serves 6–8
6-pound leg of lamb
4 garlic cloves, halved
4 tablespoons olive oil
juice of 1 lemon
2–3 saffron strands, soaked in
   1 tablespoon boiling water
1 teaspoon dried mixed herbs
1 pound potatoes
2 large onions
salt and freshly ground black pepper
fresh parsley, to garnish

1 Make several incisions in the meat and press the garlic halves into the slits. Blend the oil, lemon juice, saffron and herbs. Rub over the meat, then set aside to marinate for 2 hours.

2 Preheat the oven to 350°F. Peel the potatoes and cut them crosswise into thick slices. Cut the onions into thick slices. Layer the potatoes and onions in a large roasting pan. Lift the lamb out of the marinade and place the marinated lamb on the top of the potatoes and onions, fat side up.

3 Pour any remaining marinade over the lamb and roast in the oven for 2 hours, basting occasionally. Remove the lamb from the oven, cover loosely with foil and leave in a warm place to rest for 10–15 minutes before carving. Serve garnished with fresh parsley.

Lamb Koutlets

Koutlets are very tasty and are popular hot at a buffet or cold as snack or for picnics.

INGREDIENTS

Makes 12–15

3 eggs
1 onion, grated
2 tablespoons chopped fresh
   parsley
1 pound new potatoes, peeled
1 pound finely ground lean lamb
1 cup dried bread crumbs
oil, for frying
salt and freshly ground black pepper
mint leaves, to garnish
pita bread and herby green salad,
   to serve

1 Beat the eggs in a large bowl, add the onion and parsley, season with salt and pepper and beat together.

2 Cook the potatoes in a saucepan of boiling salted water for 20 minutes, until tender, then drain and set aside to cool. When the potatoes are cold, grate them coarsely and stir into the egg mixture together with the ground lamb. Knead by hand for 3–4 minutes until thoroughly blended.

3 Take a handful of meat and roll it into a ball. Roll the balls in the bread crumbs and then mold them into triangles, about 5 inches long. Coat with the bread crumbs again.

4 Heat the oil in a frying pan and fry the *koutlets* over a medium heat for 8–12 minutes until golden brown, turning occasionally. Serve hot, garnished with mint and accompanied by pita bread and salad.

Dill and Fava Bean Meatballs

Here's another recipe for *kofta*, *Kofta Baghali*, this time using lean ground beef instead of the more common lamb.

INGREDIENTS

Serves 4

½ cup long grain rice
1 pound ground lean beef
1 cup flour
3 eggs, beaten
1 cup fava beans, skinned
2 tablespoons chopped fresh dill
2 tablespoons butter
   or margarine
1 large onion, chopped
½ teaspoon ground turmeric
5 cups water
salt and freshly ground black pepper
chopped fresh parsley, to garnish
nan bread, to serve

1 Put the rice in a pan of water and boil for about 4 minutes until half cooked. Drain and place in a bowl with the meat, flour, eggs and seasoning. Knead thoroughly by hand until well blended.

2 Add the skinned fava beans and dill and knead again thoroughly until the mixture is firm and pasty. Shape the mixture into large balls and set aside on a plate.

3 Melt the butter or margarine in a large saucepan or flameproof casserole and fry the onion for 3–4 minutes until golden. Stir in the turmeric, cook for 30 seconds and then add the water and bring to a boil.

4 Add the meatballs to the pan, reduce the heat and simmer for 45–60 minutes until the gravy is reduced to about 1 cup. Garnish with fresh parsley and serve with nan bread.

Lamb Couscous

Couscous can be served with all sorts of different stews. This is a popular dish from Morocco.

INGREDIENTS

Serves 4

2 tablespoons oil
1 large onion
1 pound lamb, cut into
    2-inch cubes
4 tomatoes, seeded and chopped
2 garlic cloves, halved
1 teaspoon ground ginger
1 teaspoon ground fennel seeds
1 teaspoon ground turmeric
½ teaspoon chili sauce (optional)
¼ cup canned chick-peas
1¼ cups couscous
2 carrots, cut into small chunks
2 zucchini, cut into small chunks
4 new potatoes, halved
salt and freshly ground black pepper

--- COOK'S TIP ---

Couscous can be successfully cooked using the microwave. Place the soaked couscous in a microwaveproof bowl, cover with plastic wrap and microwave on medium for 5–6 minutes until tender.

1 Heat 2 tablespoons of the oil in a large saucepan and fry the onion for 4–5 minutes until softened. Add the meat and fry over a moderate heat until evenly browned all over.

2 Place the tomatoes, garlic, ginger, fennel, turmeric and chili sauce, if using, in a blender or food processor and blend to a smooth paste.

3 Pour the tomato paste over the meat, add the chick-peas and 1 cup water and bring to a boil. Season with salt and pepper. Reduce the heat, cover the pan and simmer gently for about 45 minutes.

4 Place the couscous in a large bowl and stir in the remaining oil and about 3⅔ cups water, rubbing the couscous through your fingers to separate the grains. Set aside for about 15 minutes.

5 Add the carrots, zucchini and potatoes to the stew and cook for another 15–20 minutes.

6 Place the couscous in a steamer or colander, making several deep holes in the surface with the handle of a wooden spoon. Set over the stew, cover tightly and steam for about 5–10 minutes, or until the couscous is hot and no longer grainy.

7 Place the couscous on a large serving plate, make a dent in the center and spoon over the lamb stew.

Meat Dumplings with Yogurt

These Lebanese meat dumplings are braised in yogurt sauce, a speciality known as *Shish Barak*.

INGREDIENTS

Serves 4

2 tablespoons oil
1 large onion, chopped
4 tablespoons pine nuts or
   chopped walnuts
1 pound ground lamb
2 tablespoons butter
3 garlic cloves, crushed
1 tablespoon chopped fresh mint
salt and freshly ground black pepper
mint leaves, to garnish
rice and green salad, to serve

For the dough

1 teaspoon salt
2 cups flour

For the yogurt sauce

8 cups plain yogurt
1 egg, beaten
1 tablespoon cornstarch, blended with
   1 tablespoon cold water
salt and white pepper

1 First make the dough: mix the salt and the flour together and then stir in enough water for the dough to hold together. Set aside to rest for 1 hour.

2 Heat the oil in a large frying pan and fry the onion for 3–4 minutes until soft. Add the pine nuts or walnuts and fry until golden. Stir in the meat and cook until brown. Season, then remove the pan from the heat.

3 Roll out the dough thinly on a floured board. Cut into small rounds 2–2½ inches in diameter. Place 1 teaspoon of filling on each one, fold the pastry over and firmly press the edges together. Bring the ends together to form a handle.

4 Meanwhile, make the yogurt sauce: pour the yogurt into a saucepan and beat in the egg and cornstarch mixture. Season with salt and white pepper and slowly bring to a boil, stirring constantly. Cook over a gentle heat until the sauce thickens and then carefully drop in the dumplings and simmer for about 20 minutes.

5 Spoon the dumplings and sauce onto warmed serving plates. Melt the butter in a small frying pan and fry the garlic until golden. Stir in the mint, cook briefly and then pour over the dumplings. Garnish with mint leaves and serve with rice and a green salad.

POULTRY
AND
GAME

Poultry and game birds are popular throughout the Middle East and are prepared in a wide variety of ways. Grilled or barbecued, stewed with nuts or fruits, threaded on kebabs or stuffed and baked, poultry is an important feature of family meals and festivities. One of the most famous dishes – Khoreshe Fesenjan *– consists of chicken portions simmered in an unusual and absolutely delicious sauce that includes walnuts and pomegranate paste. Another version of* khoresh, *this time with eggplant and peppers, makes a colorful contribution to the table, while roast turkey, stuffed with prunes, dried apricots, nuts and rice, is irresistible.*

Persian Chicken with Walnut Sauce

This distinctive dish, *Khoreshe Fesenjan*, is traditionally served on festive occasions in Iran.

INGREDIENTS

Serves 4
2 tablespoons oil
4 chicken pieces (leg or breast)
1 large onion, grated
1 cup water
1 cup finely chopped walnuts
5 tablespoons pomegranate paste
1 tablespoon tomato paste
2 tablespoons lemon juice
1 tablespoon sugar
3–4 saffron strands dissolved in
    1 tablespoon boiling water
salt and freshly ground black pepper
Persian rice and salad leaves,
    to serve

1 Heat 1 tablespoon of the oil in a large saucepan or flameproof casserole and sauté the chicken pieces until golden brown. Add half of the grated onion and fry until slightly softened, then add the water and seasoning and bring to a boil. Cover the pan, reduce the heat and simmer for 15 minutes.

2 Heat the remaining oil in a small saucepan or frying pan and fry the rest of the onion for 2–3 minutes until soft. Add the chopped walnuts and fry for another 2–3 minutes over a low heat, stirring frequently and taking care that the walnuts do not burn.

3 Stir in the pomegranate and tomato pastes, lemon juice, sugar and the dissolved saffron. Season to taste and then simmer over a low heat for 5 minutes.

4 Pour the walnut sauce over the chicken, making sure that all the pieces are well covered. Cover and simmer for 30–35 minutes until the meat is cooked and the oil of the walnuts has risen to the top.

5 Serve at once with Persian rice and salad leaves.

COOK'S TIP

Pomegranate paste is available from Middle Eastern delicatessens.

Chicken and Eggplant Khoresh

In Persian or Farsi this dish is known as *Khoreshe Bademjun*, *khoresh* meaning stew and *bademjun* meaning eggplant. It is often served on festive occasions and is believed to have been a favorite of kings.

INGREDIENTS

Serves 4
2 tablespoons oil
1 whole chicken or 4 large
  chicken pieces
1 large onion, chopped
2 garlic cloves, crushed
14-ounce can chopped tomatoes
1 cup water
3 eggplants, sliced
3 bell peppers, preferably red, green
  and yellow, seeded and sliced
2 tablespoons lemon juice
1 tablespoon ground cinnamon
salt and freshly ground black pepper
Persian rice, to serve

1 Heat 1 tablespoon of the oil in a large saucepan or flameproof casserole and fry the chicken or chicken pieces on both sides for about 10 minutes. Add the onion and fry for another 4–5 minutes, until the onion is golden brown.

2 Add the garlic, the chopped tomatoes and their liquid, water and seasoning. Bring to a boil, then reduce the heat and simmer slowly, covered, for 10 minutes.

3 Meanwhile, heat the remaining oil and fry the eggplant in batches until light golden. Transfer to a plate with a slotted spoon. Add the peppers to the pan and fry for a few minutes until slightly softened.

4 Place the eggplant over the chicken or chicken pieces and then add the peppers. Sprinkle over the lemon juice and cinnamon, then cover and continue cooking over a low heat for about 45 minutes, or until the chicken is cooked.

5 Transfer the chicken to a serving plate and spoon the eggplant and peppers around the edge. Reheat the sauce if necessary, adjust the seasoning and pour over the chicken. Serve the *khoresh* with Persian rice.

Chicken Kebabs

Chicken kebabs are prepared in very much the same way all over the Middle East and are a great favorite everywhere. They are ideal for barbecues on hot summer evenings.

INGREDIENTS

Serves 6–8
2 young chickens
1 large onion, grated
2 garlic cloves, crushed
½ cup olive oil
juice of 1 lemon
1 teaspoon paprika
2–3 saffron strands, soaked in
   1 tablespoon boiling water
salt and freshly ground black pepper
nan or pita bread, to serve

1 Cut the chicken into small pieces, removing the bone if preferred, and place in a shallow bowl. Mix the onion, garlic, olive oil, lemon juice, paprika and saffron, and season with salt and pepper.

2 Pour the marinade over the chicken, turning the chicken so that all the pieces are covered evenly. Cover the bowl loosely with plastic wrap and set aside in a cool place to marinate for at least 2 hours.

3 Thread the chicken onto long, preferably metal, skewers. If barbecuing, once the coals are ready, cook for 10–15 minutes, turning occasionally. Or, if you prefer, cook under a moderately hot broiler for 10–15 minutes, turning occasionally.

4 Serve with nan or pita bread. Or you could remove boneless chicken from the skewers and serve it in pita bread as a sandwich accompanied by a garlicky yogurt sauce.

Baked Rock Cornish Hens

This dish is ideal for dinner parties. It is easy to make and tasty too. Allow ample time to make this recipe, however. The Rock Cornish hens should be allowed to marinate overnight to make them extra delicious.

INGREDIENTS

Serves 4
2 cups plain yogurt
4 tablespoons olive oil
1 large onion, grated
2 garlic cloves, crushed
½ teaspoon paprika
2–3 saffron strands, soaked in
   1 tablespoon boiling water
juice of 1 lemon
4 Rock Cornish hens, halved
salt and freshly ground black pepper
Romaine lettuce salad, to serve

1 Blend together the yogurt, olive oil, onion, garlic, paprika, saffron and lemon juice, and season with salt and pepper.

2 Place the Rock Cornish hen halves in a shallow dish, pour over the marinade and then cover and allow to marinate overnight in a cool place or for at least 4 hours in the fridge.

3 Preheat the oven to 350°F. Arrange the Rock Cornish hens in a greased baking pan and bake in the oven for 30–45 minutes, basting frequently until cooked. Serve with Romaine lettuce salad.

> —— COOK'S TIP ——
>
> The hens can also be barbecued, for an authentic and even more delicious taste.

Stuffed Spring Chickens

This dish is widely found in the Lebanon and Syria. The stuffing is a delicious blend of meat, nuts and rice and makes a great dinner party dish.

INGREDIENTS

Serves 6–8
2 x 2¼-pound chickens
1 tablespoon butter
yogurt and salad, to serve

For the stuffing
3 tablespoons oil
1 onion, chopped
1 pound ground lamb
¾ cup almonds, chopped
¾ cup pine nuts
2 cups cooked rice
salt and freshly ground black pepper

1 Preheat the oven to 350°F. If necessary, remove the giblets from the chickens and rinse the body cavities in cold water.

2 Heat the oil in a large frying pan and sauté the onion until slightly softened. Add the ground lamb and cook over a moderate heat for 4–8 minutes until well browned, stirring frequently. Set aside.

3 Heat a small pan over a moderate heat and dry-fry the almonds and pine nuts for 2–3 minutes until golden, shaking the pan frequently.

4 Mix together the meat mixture, almonds, pine nuts and cooked rice. Season with salt and pepper, and then spoon the mixture into the body cavities of the chickens. Rub the chickens all over with the butter.

5 Place the chickens in a large roasting dish, cover with foil and bake in the oven for 45–60 minutes. After about 30 minutes, remove the foil and baste the chickens with the pan juices. Continue cooking without the foil until the chickens are cooked through and the meat juices run clear. Serve the chickens, cut into portions, with yogurt and a salad.

Chicken and Olives

INGREDIENTS

Serves 4

2 tablespoons olive oil
3–3½-pound chicken
1 large onion, sliced
1 tablespoon fresh root ginger, grated
3 garlic cloves, crushed
1 teaspoon paprika
1 cup chicken stock
2–3 saffron strands, soaked in 1 tablespoon boiling water
4–5 scallions, chopped
15–20 black and green olives, pitted
juice of ½ lemon
salt and freshly ground black pepper

1 Heat the oil in a large saucepan or flameproof casserole and sauté the chicken on both sides until golden.

2 Add the onion, ginger, garlic, paprika, and seasoning and continue frying over a moderate heat, coating the chicken with the mixture.

3 Add the chicken stock and saffron and bring to a boil. Cover and simmer gently for 45 minutes, or until the chicken is well done.

4 Add the scallions and cook for another 15 minutes until the chicken is well cooked and the sauce is reduced to about ½ cup.

5 Add the olives and lemon juice and cook for another 5 minutes.

6 Place the chicken on a large deep plate and pour over the sauce. Serve with rice and a mixed salad.

Persian Chicken

INGREDIENTS

Serves 4

1 tablespoon oil
4 chicken pieces
1 large onion, chopped
3 garlic cloves, finely chopped
1 teaspoon ground cinnamon
2–3 saffron strands, soaked in
  1 tablespoon boiling water
2 tablespoons lemon juice
2 cups water
salt and freshly ground black pepper
Persian rice, yogurt and salad,
  to serve

1 Heat the oil in a large saucepan or flameproof casserole and sauté the chicken pieces until golden.

2 Remove the chicken pieces from the pan or casserole. Add the onion and fry gently over a moderate heat for about 5 minutes, stirring frequently, until softened and golden, then add the garlic and fry briefly.

3 Stir in the cinnamon, saffron and lemon juice and seasoning. Return the chicken to the pan, add the water and bring to a boil. Reduce the heat, cover and simmer for 30–45 minutes until the chicken is cooked and the sauce reduced to ½ cup. Serve with rice, yogurt and salad.

Stuffed Roast Turkey

INGREDIENTS

Serves 6–8

12–14-pound turkey
juice of 2 lemons
2 tablespoons olive oil
roast potatoes and vegetables, to serve

For the stuffing

1 tablespoon butter
1 large onion, chopped
1¼ cups prunes, pitted
  and chopped
1¼ cups dried apricots, soaked and
  chopped
⅓ cup seedless raisins (optional)
1½ cups chopped mixed nuts, such as
  walnuts, almonds, pine nuts and
  pistachios
2 cups rice, cooked
1 teaspoon ground cinnamon
1 teaspoon ground turmeric
2–3 saffron strands, soaked in
  1 tablespoon boiling water
salt and freshly ground black pepper

1 Preheat the oven to 325°F. Melt the butter in a large saucepan or flameproof casserole and sauté the onion for 3–4 minutes until just slightly softened. Add the chopped prunes and apricots, and the raisins, if using, and continue frying for about 2 minutes. Stir in the nuts and fry for another 2–3 minutes then add the rice, spices and seasoning and blend well.

2 Loosely stuff the neck cavity of the turkey with the mixture, and lightly sew the openings with strong thread. Weigh the turkey in order to calculate cooking times.

3 Rub the bird with salt and pepper, place in a large roasting pan and roast in the oven for 20 minutes per 1 pound, basting frequently with lemon juice and olive oil. Serve with roast potatoes and cooked vegetables or rice and salad, if you prefer.

COOK'S TIP

This spicy, fruit- and nut-stuffed roast turkey makes an excellent alternative for a festive meal and is delicious served with either *Shirin Polo* (sweet rice), or the more traditional roast potatoes and vegetables.

FISH DISHES

One of the finest ways of enjoying fish is to grill it over hot charcoal, a cooking method which is used with excellent results all over the Middle East. Red mullet, salmon trout, sole and swordfish are popular varieties, along with cod, sardines, tuna and white fish. Salted and dried fish are Iranian specialties and are traditionally served with a special herb rice for Persian New Year. The world's finest caviar, beluga, comes from the Caspian Sea, which borders Iran to the north.

Shrimp in Tomato Sauce

Shrimp are popular everywhere in the Middle East. This delicious recipe is an easy way of making the most of them.

INGREDIENTS

Serves 4

2 tablespoons oil
2 onions, finely chopped
2–3 garlic cloves, crushed
5–6 tomatoes, peeled and chopped
2 tablespoons tomato paste
½ cup fish stock
   or water
½ teaspoon ground cumin
½ teaspoon ground cinnamon
1 pound raw, peeled medium to
   large shrimp
juice of 1 lemon
salt and freshly ground black pepper
fresh parsley, to garnish
rice, to serve

1 Heat the oil in a large frying pan or saucepan and fry the onions for 3–4 minutes until golden. Add the garlic, fry for about 1 minute, and then stir in the tomatoes.

2 Blend the tomato paste with the stock or water and stir into the pan with the cumin, cinnamon and seasoning. Simmer, covered, over a low heat for 15 minutes, stirring occasionally. Do not allow to boil.

3 Add the shrimp and lemon juice and simmer the sauce for another 10–15 minutes over a low to moderate heat until the shrimp are cooked and the stock is reduced by about half.

4 Serve with plain rice or in a decorative ring of Persian rice, garnished with parsley.

Swordfish Kebabs

Fish is most delicious when cooked over hot charcoal.

INGREDIENTS

Serves 4–6

2 pounds swordfish steaks
3 tablespoons olive oil
juice of ½ lemon
1 garlic clove, crushed
1 teaspoon paprika
3 tomatoes, quartered
2 onions, cut into wedges
salt and freshly ground black pepper
salad and pita bread, to serve

> —— COOK'S TIP ——
>
> Almost any type of firm white fish can be used for this recipe.

1 Cut the fish into large cubes and place in a dish.

2 Blend together the oil, lemon juice, garlic, paprika and seasoning in a small mixing bowl and pour over the fish. Cover loosely with plastic wrap and set aside to marinate in a cool place for up to 2 hours.

3 Thread the fish cubes onto skewers, alternating with pieces of tomato and onion.

4 Grill the kebabs over hot charcoal for 5–10 minutes, basting frequently with the remaining marinade and turning occasionally. Serve with salad and pita bread.

Tahini Baked Fish

This simple dish is a great favorite in many Arab countries, particularly Egypt, the Lebanon and Syria.

INGREDIENTS

Serves 6
6 cod or haddock fillets
juice of 2 lemons
4 tablespoons olive oil
2 large onions, chopped
1 cup tahini
1 garlic clove, crushed
3–4 tablespoons water
salt and freshly ground black pepper
rice and salad, to serve

1 Preheat the oven to 350°F. Arrange the cod or haddock fillets in a shallow casserole or bakng dish, pour over 1 tablespoon each of the lemon juice and olive oil and bake in the oven for 20 minutes.

2 Meanwhile heat the remaining oil in a large frying pan and fry the onions for 6–8 minutes until well browned and almost crisp.

3 Put the tahini, garlic and seasoning in a small bowl and slowly beat in the remaining lemon juice and water, a little at a time, until the sauce is light and creamy.

4 Sprinkle the onions over the fish, pour over the tahini sauce and bake for another 15 minutes, until the fish is cooked through and the sauce is bubbling. Serve the fish at once with rice and a salad.

Baked Fish with Nuts

This specialty comes from Egypt and is as delicious as it is unusual.

INGREDIENTS

Serves 4

3 tablespoons oil
4 small porgy, about 2 pounds in all
1 large onion, finely chopped
¾ cup hazelnuts, chopped
¾ cup pine nuts
3–4 tomatoes, sliced
3–4 tablespoons finely chopped
    fresh parsley
1 cup fish stock
salt and freshly ground black pepper
parsley sprigs, to garnish
new potatoes or rice, and vegetables or
    salad, to serve

1 Preheat the oven to 375°F. Heat 2 tablespoons of the oil in a frying pan and fry the fish, two at a time, until crisp on both sides.

2 Heat the remaining oil in a large saucepan or flameproof casserole and fry the onion for 3–4 minutes until golden. Add the chopped hazelnuts and pine nuts and stir-fry for a few minutes.

3 Stir in the tomatoes, cook for a few minutes and then add the parsley, seasoning and stock and simmer for 10–15 minutes, stirring occasionally.

COOK'S TIP

Other small whole fish, such as snapper, sea perch or butterfish, can be used for this recipe if porgy is unavailable.

---

4 Place the fish in a shallow casserole and spoon the sauce over. Bake in the oven for 20 minutes or until the fish is cooked through and flakes easily if pierced with a fork.

5 Serve the fish at once accompanied by new potatoes or rice, and vegetables or salad.

Fish with Herb Rice

INGREDIENTS

Serves 4

2–3 saffron strands
2 egg yolks
1 garlic clove, crushed
4 salmon trout steaks
oil, for deep frying
salt and freshly ground black pepper
Rice with Fresh Herbs and green salad,
     to serve

1 Soak the saffron in 1 tablespoon boiling water and then beat the mixture into the egg yolks. Season with garlic, salt and pepper.

COOK'S TIP

Any type of fish can be used in this recipe. Try a combination of plain and smoked for a delicious change, such as salmon or smoked and unsmoked cod.

---

2 Place the fish steaks in a shallow dish and coat with the egg mixture. Cover with plastic wrap and marinate for up to 1 hour.

3 Heat the oil in a deep fryer until it's very hot and then fry the fish, one steak at a time, for about 10 minutes until golden brown. Drain each one on paper towels. Serve with Rice with Fresh Herbs, lemon wedges and a green salad.

Pan-fried Sardines

This delicious fish recipe is a favorite in many Arab countries.

INGREDIENTS

Serves 4

1 tablespoon fresh parsley
3–4 garlic cloves, crushed
8–12 sardines, prepared
2 tablespoons lemon juice
½ cup flour
½ teaspoon ground cumin
4 tablespoons vegetable oil
salt and freshly ground black pepper
nan bread and salad, to serve

COOK'S TIP

Fresh sardines can be found in Portuguese markets and frozen fish are quite common in good supermarkets.

1 Finely chop the parsley and mix in a small bowl with the garlic.

2 Pat the parsley and garlic mixture all over the outsides and insides of the sardines. Sprinkle them with the lemon juice and set aside, covered, in a cool place for about 2 hours to absorb the flavors.

3 Place the flour on a large plate and season with cumin, salt and pepper. Roll the sardines in the flour, taking care to coat each fish thoroughly.

4 Heat the oil in a large frying pan and fry the fish in batches for 5 minutes on each side until crisp. Keep warm in the oven while cooking the remaining fish and then serve with nan bread and salad.

Fish with Rice

This Arabic fish dish, *Sayadieh,* is very popular in the Lebanon.

INGREDIENTS

Serves 4–6

juice of 1 lemon
3 tablespoons oil
2 pounds cod steaks
4 large onions, chopped
1 teaspoon ground cumin
2–3 saffron strands
4 cups fish stock
2⅔ cups basmati or other long grain rice
½ cup pine nuts, lightly toasted
salt and freshly ground black pepper
fresh parsley, to garnish

— COOK'S TIP —

Take care when cooking the rice that the saucepan does not boil dry. Check it occasionally and add more stock or water if it becomes necessary.

---

1 Blend together the lemon juice and 1 tablespoon of the oil in a shallow dish. Add the fish steaks, turning to coat thoroughly, then cover and set aside to marinate for 30 minutes.

2 Heat the remaining oil in a large saucepan or flameproof casserole and fry the onions for 5–6 minutes until golden, stirring occasionally.

3 Drain the fish, reserving the marinade, and add to the pan. Fry for 1–2 minutes each side until lightly golden, then add the cumin, saffron strands and a little salt and pepper.

4 Pour in the fish stock and the reserved marinade, bring to a boil and then simmer very gently over a low heat for 5–10 minutes until the fish is nearly done.

5 Transfer the fish to a plate and add the rice to the stock. Bring to a boil and then reduce the heat and simmer very gently over a low heat for 15 minutes until nearly all the stock has been absorbed.

6 Arrange the fish on the rice and cover. Steam over a low heat for another 15–20 minutes.

7 Transfer the fish to a plate, then spoon the rice onto a large flat dish and arrange the fish on top. Sprinkle with toasted pine nuts and garnish with fresh parsley.

Turkish Cold Fish

Cold fish dishes are much appreciated in the Middle East and for good reason – they are delicious! This particular version from Turkey can be made using mackerel, if preferred.

INGREDIENTS

Serves 4

4 tablespoons olive oil
2 pounds porgy or snapper
2 onions, sliced
1 green bell pepper, seeded and sliced
1 red bell pepper, seeded and sliced
3 garlic cloves, crushed
1 tablespoon tomato paste
¼ cup fish stock, bottled clam juice
   or water
5–6 tomatoes, peeled and sliced or
   14-ounce can tomatoes
2 tablespoons chopped fresh parsley
2 tablespoons lemon juice
1 teaspoon paprika
15–20 green and black olives
salt and freshly ground black pepper
bread and salad, to serve

1 Heat 2 tablespoons of the oil in a large roasting pan or frying pan and fry the fish on both sides until golden brown. Remove from the tin or pan, cover and keep warm.

> ──────── COOK'S TIP ────────
>
> One large fish looks spectacular, but it is tricky to both cook and serve. If you prefer, buy four smaller fish and cook for a shorter time, until just tender and cooked through but not overdone.

2 Heat the remaining oil in the pan and fry the onion for 2–3 minutes until slightly softened. Add the green and red peppers and continue cooking for 3–4 minutes, stirring occasionally, then add the garlic and stir-fry for another minute.

3 Blend the tomato paste with the fish stock, clam juice or water and stir into the pan with the tomatoes, parsley, lemon juice, paprika and seasoning. Simmer very gently for 15 minutes, stirring occasionally.

4 Return the fish to the pan and cover with the sauce. Cook for 10 minutes, then add the olives and cook for another 5 minutes or until just cooked through.

5 Transfer the fish to a serving dish and pour the sauce over the top. Allow to cool, then cover and chill until completely cold. Serve cold with bread and salad.

RICE AND VEGETABLES

Rice in some form is served at almost every Middle Eastern meal, from plain boiled and buttered Iranian Chelo to elaborate combinations of rice, meat, vegetables and nuts. Polo resembles a pilaf, in that the accompaniments are mixed in and cooked with the rice. Rice is very easy to prepare and the Persian method gives particularly good results. When rice is cooked this way, a crisp golden crust forms at the bottom; this is the tahdiq, *regarded by many as the best part of the rice. Stuffed vegetables, salads and a delicious soufflé round off this chapter.*

Persian Rice

Plain rice in Iran is called *Chelo*. The rice is soaked in salted water before cooking. Don't skimp on this process – the longer it is soaked, the better the flavour of the finished rice.

INGREDIENTS
Serves 4
scant 2 cups long
  grain rice
about 4 teaspoons salt
3 tablespoons melted butter
2–3 saffron strands, soaked in
  1 tablespoon boiling water (optional)

1 Soak the rice in lukewarm water, salted with 1 tablespoon salt for a minimum of two hours.

2 When the rice has soaked, and you are ready to cook, fill a nonstick pan with fresh water, add a little salt and bring to a boil.

3 Drain the rice and stir into the boiling water. Boil for 5 minutes, then reduce the heat and simmer for about 10 minutes until half cooked. Drain and rinse in lukewarm water. Wash and dry the pan.

4 Heat 2 tablespoons of the melted butter in the saucepan. Make sure you do not overcook it or it will burn. Add about 1 tablespoon water and stir in the rice. Cook the rice over a very low heat for 10 minutes, then pour over the remaining butter.

5 Cover the pan with a clean dish towel and secure with a tightly fitting lid, lifting the corners of the cloth back over the lid.

6 Steam the rice for 30–40 minutes. The cloth will absorb the excess steam and will turn the bottom of the rice into a crisp, golden crust called *tahdiq*. This is regarded by many as the best part of the rice. To serve, if you like, mix 2–3 tablespoons of the rice with the saffron water and sprinkle over the top of the rice.

Plain Rice

This is a simplified and quicker version of Persian Rice (*Chelo*).

INGREDIENTS

Serves 4
3²⁄₃ cups water
1 teaspoon salt
scant 2 cups basmati rice
3 tablespoons butter

1 Place the water and salt in a nonstick saucepan and pour in the rice. Set aside to soak for at least 30 minutes and for up to 2 hours.

2 Bring the water and rice to the boil, then reduce the heat and simmer for 10–15 minutes until the water is absorbed.

3 Add the butter to the rice, cover the pan with a tightly fitting lid and steam over a very low heat for about 30 minutes. Serve with *Khoresh*, or any other meat dish.

Sweet and Sour Rice

Zereshk Polo is flavored with fruit and spices and is commonly served with chicken dishes.

INGREDIENTS

Serves 4

2 ounces *zereshk*
3 tablespoons melted butter
⅓ cup raisins
2 tablespoons sugar
1 teaspoon ground cinnamon
1 teaspoon ground cumin
scant 2 cups basmati rice, soaked in
   salted water for 2 hours
2–3 saffron strands, soaked in
   1 tablespoon boiling water
salt

1 Thoroughly wash the *zereshk* in cold water at least 4–5 times to rinse off any bits of grit.

2 Heat 1 tablespoon of the butter in a small frying pan and stir-fry the raisins for 1–2 minutes.

3 Add the *zereshk*, fry for a few seconds and then add the sugar, and half of the cinnamon and cumin. Cook briefly and then set aside.

4 Drain the rice and then boil in a saucepan in salted water for 5 minutes, reduce the heat and simmer for 10 minutes until half cooked.

5 Drain and rinse in lukewarm water and wash and dry the pan. Heat half of the remaining butter in the pan, add 1 tablespoon water and stir in half of the rice.

6 Sprinkle with half of the raisin and *zereshk* mixture and top with all but 3 tablespoons of the rice. Sprinkle over the remaining raisin mixture.

7 Blend the reserved rice with the remaining cinnamon and cumin and sprinkle over the top of the rice mixture. Drizzle the remaining butter over and then cover the pan with a clean dish towel and secure with a tightly fitting lid, lifting the corners of the cloth back over the lid. Steam the rice over a very low heat for about 30–40 minutes.

8 Just before serving, mix about 3 tablespoons of the rice with the saffron water. Spoon the rice on to a large flat serving dish and sprinkle the saffron rice over the top to decorate.

COOK'S TIP

Zereshk are very small dried berries that are delicious mixed with rice. They are available from most Persian and Middle Eastern food stores.

Rice with Dill and Fava Beans

This is another favorite rice dish from Iran where it is called *Baghali Polo*.

INGREDIENTS

Serves 4

1½ cups basmati rice, soaked in salted
  water for 3 hours
3 tablespoons melted butter
1½ cups fava beans, skinned fresh
  or frozen
6 tablespoons finely chopped fresh dill
1 teaspoon ground cinnamon
1 teaspoon ground cumin
2–3 saffron strands, soaked in
  1 tablespoon boiling water
salt

1 Drain the rice and then boil in salted water for 5 minutes. Reduce the heat and simmer very gently for 10 minutes until half cooked. Drain and rinse in lukewarm water.

2 Put 1 tablespoon of the melted butter in a nonstick saucepan and then add enough rice to cover the bottom of the pan. Add a quarter of the fava beans and a little of the dill.

3 Add another layer of rice, followed by a layer of fava beans and dill and continue making layers until all the beans and dill are used, finishing with a layer of rice.

4 Cook over a gentle heat for 10 minutes. Pour the remaining melted butter over the rice.

5 Sprinkle the cinnamon and cumin evenly over the top of the rice. Cover the pan with a clean dish towel and secure with a tightly fitting lid, lifting the corners of the cloth back over the lid, and then steam over a very low heat for 30–45 minutes.

6 Mix 3 tablespoons of the rice with the saffron water. Spoon the remaining rice onto a large serving plate and sprinkle over the saffron rice to decorate. Serve with either a lamb or chicken dish.

Sweet Rice

In Iran, sweet rice, *Shirin Polo,* is always served at wedding banquets and on other traditional special occasions.

INGREDIENTS

Serves 8–10
3 oranges
6 tablespoons sugar
3 tablespoons melted butter
5–6 carrots, cut into julienne strips
½ cup mixed chopped pistachios, almonds and pine nuts
3½ cups basmati rice, soaked in salted water for 2 hours
2–3 saffron strands, soaked in 1 tablespoon boiling water
salt

COOK'S TIP

Take care to cook this rice over a very low heat as it can burn easily owing to the sugar in the carrots.

1 Cut the peel from the oranges in wide strips using a potato peeler, and cut the peel into thin shreds.

2 Place the strips of peel in a saucepan with enough water to cover and bring to a boil. Simmer for a few minutes, drain and repeat this process until you have removed the bitter flavor of the peel.

3 Place the peel back in the pan with 3 tablespoons of the sugar and 4 tablespoons water. Bring to a boil and then simmer until the water is reduced by half. Set aside.

4 Heat 1 tablespoon of the butter in a pan and fry the carrots for 2–3 minutes. Add the remaining sugar and 4 tablespoons water and simmer for 10 minutes until almost evaporated.

5 Stir the carrots and half of the nuts into the orange peel and set aside. Drain the rice, boil in salted water for 5 minutes, then reduce the heat and simmer very gently for 10 minutes until half cooked. Drain and rinse.

6 Heat 1 tablespoon of the remaining butter in the pan and add about 3 tablespoons water. Fork a little of the rice into the pan and spoon on some of the orange mixture. Make layers until all the mixture has been used.

7 Cook gently for 10 minutes. Pour over the remaining butter and cover with a clean dish towel. Secure with a lid and steam for 30–45 minutes. Serve garnished with the remaining nuts and the saffron water.

Rice with Fresh Herbs

INGREDIENTS

Serves 4
scant 2 cups basmati rice, soaked in salted water for 2 hours
2 tablespoons finely chopped fresh parsley
2 tablespoons finely chopped fresh cilantro
2 tablespoons finely chopped fresh chives
1 tablespoon finely chopped fresh dill
3–4 scallions, finely chopped
4 tablespoons butter
1 teaspoon ground cinnamon
2–3 saffron strands, soaked in 1 tablespoon boiling water
salt

1 Drain the rice, and then boil in salted water for 5 minutes, reduce the heat and simmer for 10 minutes.

2 Stir in the herbs and scallions and mix well with a fork. Simmer for a few minutes more, then drain but do not rinse. Wash and dry the pan.

3 Heat half of the butter in the pan, add 1 tablespoon water, then stir in the rice. Cook over a very low heat for 10 minutes, then test to see if it is half cooked. Add the remaining butter, the cinnamon and saffron water and cover the pan with a clean dish towel. Secure with a tightly fitting lid, and steam over a very low heat for 30–40 minutes.

Green Beans, Rice and Beef

INGREDIENTS

Serves 4

2 tablespoons butter or margarine
1 large onion, chopped
1 pound stewing beef, cubed
2 garlic cloves, crushed
1 teaspoon ground cinnamon
1 teaspoon ground cumin powder
1 teaspoon ground turmeric
1 pound tomatoes, chopped
2 tablespoons tomato paste
1½ cups water
12 ounces green beans
salt and freshly ground black pepper

For the rice

1½ cups basmati rice, soaked in salted
  water for 2 hours
7½ cups water
3 tablespoons melted butter
2–3 saffron strands, soaked in
  1 tablespoon boiling water
salt

1 Melt the butter or margarine in a large saucepan or flameproof casserole and fry the onion until golden. Add the meat and fry until evenly brown, and then add the garlic, spices, tomatoes, tomato paste and water. Season with salt and pepper. Bring to a boil, then reduce the heat and simmer over a low heat for about 30 minutes.

2 Cut the green beans into pieces and add to the meat.

3 Continue cooking the beans for another 15 minutes until the meat is tender and most of the meat juices have evaporated.

4 Meanwhile, prepare the rice. Drain and then boil the rice in salted water for 5 minutes, reduce the heat and simmer very gently for about 10 minutes until half cooked. Drain and rinse the rice in warm water. Wash and dry the pan.

5 Heat 1 tablespoon of the melted butter in the pan and stir in about a third of the rice.

6 Spoon half of the meat mixture over the rice, add a layer of rice, the remaining meat and finish with a layer of rice.

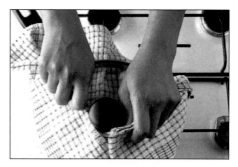

7 Pour the remaining melted butter over the rice and cover the pan with a clean dish towel. Cover with a tightly fitting lid and steam for about 30–45 minutes over a low heat.

8 Take 3 tablespoons rice and mix with the saffron water. Serve the rice on a large flat dish and sprinkle the saffron rice on top.

Yogurt Chicken and Rice

This rice dish, *Tah Chin*, is very unusual and tastes superb.

INGREDIENTS

Serves 6
3 tablespoons butter
3–3½-pound chicken
1 large onion, chopped
1 cup chicken stock
2 eggs
2 cups plain yogurt
2–3 saffron strands, dissolved in
   1 tablespoon boiling water
1 teaspoon ground cinnamon
2 cups basmati rice
3 ounces *zereshk*
salt and freshly ground black pepper
herb salad, to serve

1 Melt 2 tablespoons of the butter and fry the chicken and onion for 4–5 minutes until the onion is softened and the chicken browned.

2 Add the chicken stock and salt and pepper, bring to a boil, then reduce the heat and simmer for about 45 minutes, or until the chicken is cooked and the stock reduced by half.

3 Skin and bone the chicken. Cut the meat into large pieces and place in a large bowl. Reserve the stock.

COOK'S TIP

If you prefer, use boned chicken breasts or thighs instead of a whole chicken. These are available at most supermarkets.

---

4 Beat the eggs and blend with the yogurt. Add the saffron water and cinnamon and season with salt and pepper. Pour over the chicken and set aside to marinate for up to 2 hours.

5 Drain the rice and then boil in salted water for 5 minutes, reduce the heat and simmer very gently for 10 minutes until half cooked. Drain and rinse in lukewarm water.

6 Transfer the chicken from the yogurt mixture to a dish and mix half the rice into the yogurt.

7 Preheat the oven to 325°F and grease a large 4-inch deep casserole or baking dish.

8 Place the rice and yogurt mixture in the bottom of the casserole or dish, arrange the chicken pieces in a layer on top and then add the plain rice. Sprinkle with the *zereshk*.

9 Mix the remaining butter with the chicken stock and pour over the rice. Cover tightly with foil and cook in the oven for 35–45 minutes.

10 Let the casserole or dish cool for a few minutes. Place on a cold, damp cloth which will help lift the rice from the bottom, then run a knife around the edges of the casserole or dish. Place a large flat plate over the top and turn out. You should have a rice "cake" which can be cut into wedges. Serve hot with a herb salad.

Eggplant Bake

Eggplants are extremely popular all over the Middle East. This particular dish, *Kuku Bademjan*, comes from Iran.

INGREDIENTS

Serves 4

4 tablespoons oil
1 onion, finely chopped
3–4 garlic cloves, crushed
4 eggplants, cut into quarters
6 eggs
2–3 saffron strands, soaked in
  1 tablespoon boiling water
1 teaspoon paprika
salt and freshly ground black pepper
chopped fresh parsley, to garnish
bread and salad, to serve

1 Preheat the oven to 350°F. Heat about 2 tablespoons of the oil in a frying pan and fry the onion until golden. Add the garlic, fry for about 2 minutes and then add the eggplants and cook for 10–12 minutes until soft and golden brown. Cool and then chop the eggplants.

2 Beat the eggs in a large bowl and stir in the eggplant mixture, saffron water, paprika and seasoning. Place the remaining oil in a deep casserole. Heat in the oven for a few minutes, then add the egg and eggplant mixture. Bake for 30–40 minutes until set. Garnish with parsley and serve with bread and salad.

Turkish-style Vegetable Casserole

INGREDIENTS

Serves 4

4 tablespoons olive oil
1 large onion, chopped
2 eggplants, cut into small cubes
4 zucchini, cut into small chunks
4–5 okra, soaked in vinegar for
  30 minutes, cut into short lengths
1 green bell pepper, seeded and
  chopped
1 red bell pepper, seeded and chopped
1 cup fresh or frozen peas
4 ounces green beans
1 pound new potatoes, cubed
½ teaspoon ground cinnamon
½ teaspoon ground cumin
1 teaspoon paprika
4–5 tomatoes, skinned
14-ounce can chopped tomatoes
2 tablespoons chopped fresh parsley
3–4 garlic cloves, crushed
1½ cups vegetable stock
salt and freshly ground black pepper
black olives, to garnish

1 Preheat the oven to 375°F. Heat 3 tablespoons of the oil in a heavy-bottomed pan and fry the onion until golden. Add the eggplants and sauté for about 3 minutes, then add the zucchini, okra, green and red bell pepper, peas, green beans and potatoes, together with the spices and seasoning. Cook for another 3 minutes, stirring all the time, then transfer the vegetable mixture to a shallow casserole.

2 Chop and seed the fresh tomatoes and mix with the canned tomatoes, parsley, garlic and the remaining olive oil in a bowl.

3 Pour the stock over the vegetables and then spoon over the tomato mixture. Cover and cook in the oven for 45–60 minutes. Serve, garnished with black olives.

Baked Stuffed Eggplant

The name of this famous Turkish *mezze* dish, *Imam Bayaldi*, literally means, "the Imam fainted" – perhaps with pleasure at the deliciousness of the dish.

INGREDIENTS

Serves 6

3 eggplants
4 tablespoons olive oil
1 large onion, chopped
2 small bell peppers (1 red and
    1 green), seeded and diced
3 garlic cloves, crushed
5–6 tomatoes, peeled and chopped
2 tablespoons chopped fresh parsley
about 1 cup boiling water
1 tablespoon lemon juice
salt and freshly ground black pepper
chopped fresh parsley, to garnish
bread, salad and yogurt dip,
    to serve

COOK'S TIP

This flavorful dish can be made in advance and is ideal for a buffet table.

1 Preheat the oven to 375°F. Cut the eggplants in half lengthwise and scoop out the flesh, reserving the shells.

2 Heat 2 tablespoons of the olive oil and fry the onion and peppers for 5–6 minutes until both are slightly softened but not too tender.

3 Add the garlic and continue to cook for another 2 minutes then stir in the tomatoes, parsley and eggplant flesh. Season and then stir well and fry over a moderate heat for 2–3 minutes.

4 Heat the remaining oil in a separate pan and fry the eggplant shells, two at a time, on both sides.

5 Stuff the shells with the sautéed vegetables. Arrange the eggplants closely together in a shallow casserole and pour enough boiling water around the eggplants to come about halfway up their sides.

6 Cover with foil and bake in the oven for 45–60 minutes until the eggplants are tender and most of the liquid has been absorbed.

7 Place a half eggplant on each serving plate and sprinkle with a little lemon juice. Serve the eggplants hot or cold, garnished with parsley and accompanied by bread, salad and a yogurt dip.

Spinach Pie

This Turkish dish, *Fatayer*, makes a healthy vegetarian dish.

INGREDIENTS

Serves 6

2 pounds fresh spinach, chopped
2 tablespoons butter or margarine
2 onions, chopped
2 garlic cloves, crushed
10 ounces feta cheese, crumbled
¾ cup pine nuts
5 eggs, beaten
2 saffron strands, soaked in
    2 tablespoons boiling water
1 teaspoon paprika
¼ teaspoon ground cumin
¼ teaspoon ground cinnamon
14 sheets filo pastry
about 4 tablespoons olive oil
salt and freshly ground black pepper
lettuce, to serve

1 Place the spinach in a large colander, sprinkle with a little salt, rub into the leaves and leave for 30 minutes to drain the excess liquid.

2 Preheat the oven to 350°F. Melt the butter or margarine in a large pan and fry the onions until golden. Add the garlic, cheese and nuts. Remove from the heat and stir in the eggs, spinach, saffron and spices. Season with salt and pepper and mix well.

COOK'S TIP

Cheddar, Parmesan or any hard cheese can be added to this dish as well as the feta.

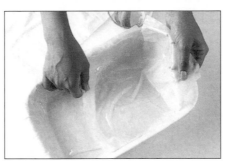

3 Grease a large rectangular baking pan. Take seven of the sheets of filo and brush one side of each with a little olive oil. Place on the bottom of the pan, overlapping the sides.

4 Spoon all of the spinach mixture over the pastry and carefully drizzle 2 tablespoons of the remaining olive oil over the top.

5 Fold the overlapping pastry over the filling. Cut the remaining pastry sheets to the pan size and brush each one with more olive oil. Arrange on top of the filling.

6 Brush with water to prevent curling and then bake in the oven for about 30 minutes, until the pastry is golden brown. Serve with the lettuce.

Tabbouleh

This classic Lebanese salad has become very popular in other countries. It makes an ideal substitute for a rice dish on a buffet table and is excellent served with cold sliced lamb.

Ingredients

Serves 4

1 cup fine bulgur wheat
juice of 1 lemon
3 tablespoons olive oil
½ cup finely chopped fresh parsley
3 tablespoons fresh mint, chopped
4–5 scallions, chopped
1 green bell pepper, seeded and sliced
salt and freshly ground black pepper
2 large tomatoes, diced, and black
   olives, to garnish

1 Put the bulgur wheat in a bowl. Add enough cold water to cover it and let it stand for at least 30 minutes and up to 2 hours.

2 Drain and squeeze with your hands to remove excess water. The bulgur wheat will swell to double the size. Spread on paper towels to dry the bulgur wheat completely.

3 Place the bulgur wheat in a large bowl, add the lemon juice, the oil and a little salt and pepper. Allow to stand for 1–2 hours if possible, in order for the flavors to develop.

4 Add the chopped parsley, mint, scallions and bell pepper and mix well. Garnish with diced tomatoes and olives and serve.

Yogurt with Cucumber

Ingredients

Serves 4–6

½ cucumber
1 small onion
2 garlic cloves
1 tablespoon fresh parsley
2 cups plain yogurt
¼ teaspoon paprika
salt and white pepper
mint leaves, to garnish

1 Finely chop the cucumber and onion, crush the garlic and finely chop the parsley.

----- COOK'S TIP -----

It's not traditional, but other herbs, such as mint or chives, would be equally good in this dish.

2 Lightly beat the yogurt and then add the cucumber, onion, garlic and parsley and season with salt and pepper to taste.

3 Sprinkle with a little paprika and chill for at least 1 hour. Garnish with mint leaves and serve with warm pita bread or as an accompaniment to meat, poultry and rice dishes.

Turkish Salad

This classic salad is a wonderful combination of textures and flavors. The saltiness of the cheese is perfectly balanced by the refreshing salad vegetables.

INGREDIENTS

Serves 4
1 Romaine lettuce heart
1 green bell pepper
1 red bell pepper
½ cucumber
4 tomatoes
1 red onion
8 ounces feta cheese, crumbled
black olives, to garnish

For the dressing
3 tablespoons olive oil
3 tablespoons lemon juice
1 garlic clove, crushed
1 tablespoon chopped fresh parsley
1 tablespoon chopped fresh mint
salt and freshly ground black pepper

1 Chop the lettuce into bite-size pieces. Seed the peppers, remove the cores and cut the flesh into thin strips. Chop the cucumber and slice or chop the tomatoes. Cut the onion in half, then slice finely.

2 Place the chopped lettuce, peppers, cucumber, tomatoes and onion in a large bowl. Sprinkle the feta over the top and toss together lightly.

3 To make the dressing: blend together the olive oil, lemon juice and garlic in a small bowl. Stir in the parsley and mint and season with salt and pepper to taste.

4 Pour the dressing over the salad, toss lightly and serve garnished with a handful of black olives.

Persian Salad

This very simple, refreshing salad can be served with almost any Persian dish – don't add the dressing until just before you are ready to serve.

INGREDIENTS

Serves 4
4 tomatoes
½ cucumber
1 onion
1 Romaine lettuce heart

For the dressing
2 tablespoons olive oil
juice of 1 lemon
1 garlic clove, crushed
salt and freshly ground black pepper

1 Cut the tomatoes and cucumber into small cubes. Finely chop the onion and tear the lettuce into pieces.

2 Place the tomatoes, cucumber, onion and lettuce in a large salad bowl and mix lightly together.

3 To make the dressing, pour the olive oil into a small bowl. Add the lemon juice, garlic and seasoning and blend together well. Pour over the salad and toss lightly to mix. Sprinkle with black pepper and serve with meat or rice dishes.

DESSERTS

The most popular dessert in the Middle East is
fruit. The cornucopia includes melons of every
type, pomegranates, figs, cherries, grapes, apricots
and peaches, served simply or as a refreshing salad
scented with rose water. Rich treats like Baklava,
Coconut Halva, and Almond Fingers are reserved
for special occasions or kept for callers – both
invited and unexpected. Traditional hospitality
demands that everyone who visits a Middle
Eastern home is offered food, so sweets
are usually baked in sufficient quantity
to make sure that no guest ever goes hungry.

Persian Melon

Called *Paludeh Garmac*, this is a typical Persian dessert, using delicious, sweet fresh fruits flavored with rose water and a hint of aromatic mint.

INGREDIENTS

Serves 4

2 small melons
1 cup strawberries, sliced
3 peaches, peeled and cut into small cubes
1 bunch of seedless grapes (green or red)
2 tablespoons sugar
1 tablespoon rose water
1 tablespoon lemon juice
crushed ice (optional)
4 sprigs of mint, to decorate

1 Carefully cut the melons in half and remove the seeds. Scoop out the flesh with a melon baller, making sure not to damage the skin. Reserve the melon shells. Alternatively, if you don't have a melon baller, scoop out the flesh using a large spoon and cut into bite-size pieces.

2 Reserve four strawberries and slice the others. Place in a bowl with the melon balls, the peaches, grapes, sugar, rose water and lemon juice.

3 Pile the fruit into the melon shells and chill in the fridge for 2 hours.

4 To serve, sprinkle with crushed ice, decorating each melon with a whole strawberry and a sprig of mint.

--- COOK'S TIP ---

To peel peaches, cover with boiling water and leave to stand for a couple of minutes. Cool under cold water before peeling.

Oranges in Syrup

This is a favorite classic dessert. It is light and simple-to-make, refreshing and delicious.

INGREDIENTS

Serves 4

4 oranges
2½ cups water
1½ cups sugar
2 tablespoons lemon juice
2 tablespoons orange blossom water or rose water
½ cup pistachio nuts, shelled and chopped

--- COOK'S TIP ---

A perfect dessert to serve after a heavy main course dish. Almonds could be substituted for the pistachio nuts, if you like.

1 Peel the oranges with a vegetable peeler down to the pith.

2 Cut the orange peel into fine strips and boil in water several times to remove the bitterness. Drain and set aside until needed.

3 Place the water, sugar and lemon juice in a saucepan. Bring to a boil and then add the orange peel and simmer until the syrup thickens. Add the orange blossom or rose water, stir and set aside to cool.

4 Completely peel the pith from the oranges and cut them into thick slices. Arrange in a shallow serving dish and pour over the syrup. Chill for about 1–2 hours and then decorate with pistachio nuts and serve.

Apple Froth

This is another very popular dessert. It is easy to make and is perfect after a rich meal.

INGREDIENTS

Serves 4

4 apples
2 tablespoons lemon juice
2 tablespoons rose water
3–4 tablespoons confectioner's sugar
crushed ice, to serve

COOK'S TIP

Pears are also excellent in this light refreshing dessert. Choose ripe pears if using them. They will yield when gently pressed at the stalk end, but take care not to bruise them.

1 Carefully and thinly cut the peel from the apples using a vegetable peeler. Discard the peel. Work quickly, otherwise the apples will begin to brown. If necessary, place the peeled apples in a bowl of lemony water while you peel the others.

2 Grate the apples coarsely into a bowl, discarding the cores, then transfer to a pretty serving dish.

3 Stir in the lemon juice, rose water and add sugar to taste.

4 Chill for at least 30 minutes and serve with crushed ice.

Pineapple Ice Cream

INGREDIENTS

Serves 8–10

8 eggs, separated
½ cup superfine sugar
½ teaspoon vanilla extract
2½ cups heavy or
   whipping cream
3–4 tablespoons confectioner's sugar,
   to taste
15-ounce can pineapple chunks
¾ cup pistachio nuts, chopped
wafer cookies, to serve

1 Place the egg yolks in a bowl, add the superfine sugar and vanilla extract and beat until thick and pale.

2 Whip the cream and confectioner's sugar to soft peaks, add to the egg yolk mixture and mix well.

3 Whisk the egg whites in a separate large bowl until they are firm and hold stiff peaks. Gently fold the egg whites into the cream mixture and blend well.

4 Cut the pineapple into very small pieces, add the pistachio nuts and stir into the cream mixture and mix well with a spoon.

5 Pour the mixture into a freezer container and place in the freezer for a few hours until it is set and firm, stirring it once or twice.

6 Cut into thick slices and serve in a pretty glass dish decorated with wafer cookies.

Baklava

This is queen of all pastries with its exotic flavors and is usually served for the Persian New Year on March 21, celebrating the first day of spring.

INGREDIENTS

Serves 6–8

3³⁄₄ cups ground
   pistachio nuts
1¹⁄₄ cups confectioner's sugar
1 tablespoon ground cardamom
about ²⁄₃ cup unsalted butter,
   melted
1 pound filo pastry

For the syrup

2 cups granulated or
   superfine sugar
1¹⁄₄ cups water
2 tablespoons rose water

1 First make the syrup: place the sugar and water in a saucepan, bring to a boil and then simmer for about 10 minutes until syrupy. Stir in the rose water and set aside to cool.

2 Mix together the pistachio nuts, confectioner's sugar and ground cardamom. Preheat the oven to 325°F and brush a large rectangular baking pan with a little melted butter.

3 Taking one sheet of filo pastry at a time, and keeping the remainder covered with a damp cloth, brush with melted butter and lay on the bottom of the pan. Continue until you have six buttered layers in the pan. Spread half of the nut mixture over, pressing down with a spoon.

4 Take another six sheets of filo pastry, brush each with butter and lay over the nut mixture. Sprinkle over the remaining nuts and top with a final layer of six filo sheets each brushed again with butter. Cut the pastry diagonally into small lozenge shapes using a sharp knife. Pour the remaining melted butter over the top.

5 Bake for 20 minutes, then increase the heat to 400°F and bake for about 15 minutes until light golden in color and puffed.

6 Remove from the oven and drizzle about three quarters of the syrup over the pastry, reserving the remainder for serving. Arrange the baklava lozenges on a large glass dish and serve with extra syrup.

Omm Ali

Here's an Egyptian version of bread and butter pudding.

INGREDIENTS

Serves 4

10–12 sheets filo pastry
2½ cups milk
1 cup heavy or whipping cream
1 egg, beaten
2 tablespoons rose water
½ cup each chopped pistachio nuts,
    almonds and hazelnuts
⅔ cup raisins
1 tablespoon ground cinnamon
light cream, to serve

1 Preheat the oven to 325°F. Bake the filo pastry, on a baking sheet, for 15–20 minutes until crisp. Remove the baking sheet from the oven and raise the temperature to 400°F.

2 Scald the milk and heavy or whipping cream by pouring into a pan and heating very gently until hot but not boiling. Slowly add the beaten egg and the rose water. Cook over a very low heat, until the mixture begins to thicken, stirring all the time.

3 Crumble the pastry using your hands and then spread in layers with the nuts and raisins into the bottom of a shallow baking dish.

4 Pour the custard mixture over the nut and pastry base and bake in the oven for 20 minutes until golden. Sprinkle with cinnamon and serve with light cream.

Café Glacé

INGREDIENTS

Serves 4–6

2–3 tablespoons instant dried coffee
2½ cups water
1 tablespoon sugar
2½ cups milk
ice cubes and vanilla ice cream,
    to serve
4–6 chocolate candy bars, to decorate
8–12 crisp wafer cookies,
    to serve

— COOK'S TIP —

You'll need to provide straws and long
spoons for eating this dessert. Adjust the
amount of coffee and sugar to suit your taste.

1 Bring ½ cup of the water to the
boil, then transfer to a small mixing
bowl and stir in the coffee. Add the
sugar and stir until it dissolves. Chill for
2 hours. Mix together the milk and the
remaining water in a large pitcher. Add
the chilled coffee and stir well.

2 Pour the coffee mixture into long
glasses until they are three quarters
full. Add ice cubes and the ice cream to
the top of each glass. Decorate with the
chocolate flakes and serve with the
wafer cookies.

Sweet Custard

This is a popular dessert in the
Arab countries. It has a smooth,
silky texture and a subtle flavor.

INGREDIENTS

Serves 4

¼ cup ground rice
3 tablespoons cornstarch
5 cups milk
6 tablespoons sugar
2 tablespoons rose water
¾ cup ground almonds
¼ cup ground pistachio nuts
ground cinnamon, to decorate
syrup or honey, melted, to serve

1 Blend the ground rice and
cornstarch to a paste with a little
cold milk in a small bowl.

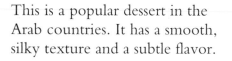

2 Bring the remaining milk to a
boil, add the sugar and simmer
gently. Gradually add the ground rice
paste to the milk, stirring constantly
with a wooden spoon to mix.

3 Simmer the mixture on a very
gentle heat for 10–15 minutes,
until the mixture has thickened, stirring
frequently and being very careful not
to burn the bottom of the pan, which
would damage the very delicate flavor
of the rice.

4 Stir in the rose water and half of
the ground almonds and simmer
for another 5 minutes.

5 Cool for a few minutes and then
pour into a serving bowl or
individual dishes. Sprinkle with the
remaining ground almonds and the
pistachio nuts and decorate with a
dusting of ground cinnamon. Serve
with melted syrup or honey.

Date and Nut Pastries

INGREDIENTS

Makes 35–40

4 cups flour
1 cup unsalted butter, cut into cubes
3 tablespoons rose water
4–5 tablespoons milk
confectioner's sugar,
    for sprinkling

For the filling

1¼ cups dates, pitted
    and chopped
1¼ cups walnuts, finely
    chopped
¾ cup blanched almonds, finely
    chopped
½ cup pistachio nuts, finely
    chopped
½ cup water
½ cup granulated sugar
2 teaspoons ground cinnamon

1 Preheat the oven to 325°F. First make the filling: place the dates, walnuts, almonds, pistachio nuts, water, granulated sugar and cinnamon in a small saucepan and cook over a low heat until the dates are soft and the water has been absorbed.

2 Place the flour in a large bowl and add the butter, working it into the flour with your fingertips.

3 Add the rose water and milk and knead the dough until it's soft.

4 Take walnut-size lumps of dough. Roll each into a ball and hollow with your thumb. Pinch the sides.

5 Place a spoonful of date mixture in the hollow and then press the dough back over the filling to seal.

6 Arrange the pastries on a large baking tray. Press to flatten them slightly. Make little dents with a fork on the pastry. Bake in the oven for 20 minutes. Do not let them change color or the pastry will become hard. Cool slightly and then sprinkle with confectioner's sugar and serve.

Yellow Rice Pudding

This baked rice pudding, *Sholezard*, is one of the most delicious desserts in all of Persia.

INGREDIENTS

Serves 6–8

1 cup short grain rice
6¼ cups water
1½ cups sugar
2–3 saffron strands, dissolved in
    1 tablespoon boiling water
4 tablespoons rose water
½ teaspoon ground cardamom
¾ cup chopped blanched
    almonds
2 tablespoons butter
¼ cup chopped pistachio nuts
1 teaspoon ground cinnamon

1 Preheat the oven to 300°F. Place the rice and water in a large pan, bring to a boil and simmer until the rice is soft and swollen.

2 Pour 1 cup water into another saucepan, add the sugar and simmer for 10 minutes. Add the saffron, rose water, cardamom and ⅓ cup of the almonds. Stir well.

3 Pour the syrup over the rice, add the butter and stir well.

--- COOK'S TIP ---

Make sure that the sugar is completely dissolved before the syrup begins to boil, then reduce the heat and simmer the syrup without stirring.

4 Pour the rice mixture into a shallow casserole, cover with a lid or with foil and bake in the oven for 30 minutes.

5 Remove the casserole from the oven and decorate with the remaining almonds and pistachio nuts, dust with cinnamon and then chill before serving or serve warm.

Almond Fingers

A very simple Middle Eastern cookie which is especially popular in Arab countries, where it is known as Zeinab's Fingers.

INGREDIENTS

Makes 40–50
2¼ cups ground almonds
½ cup ground pistachio nuts
¼ cup granulated sugar
1 tablespoon rose water
½ teaspoon ground cinnamon
12 sheets of filo pastry
½ cup melted unsalted butter
confectioner's sugar, for dusting

1 Preheat the oven to 325°F. Mix together the nuts, sugar, rose water and cinnamon for the filling.

2 Cut each sheet of filo pastry into four rectangles. Work with one rectangle at a time, and cover the remaining rectangles with a damp dish towel to prevent them from drying.

3 Brush one of the rectangles of filo pastry with a little melted butter and place a heaped teaspoon of the nut filling in the center.

4 Fold in the sides and roll into a finger or cigar shape. Continue making "cigars" until all the filling has been used.

5 Place the fingers on a buttered baking sheet and bake in the oven for 30 minutes or until light golden.

6 Remove and cool and then dust with confectioner's sugar.

Coconut Halva

This delicious coconut cake, traditionally called *Basbousa*, can be served either hot as a dessert or cold with tea.

INGREDIENTS

Serves 4–6
½ cup unsalted butter
¾ cup sugar
½ cup flour
1¼ cups semolina
1½ cups grated coconut
¾ cup milk
1 teaspoon baking powder
1 teaspoon vanilla extract
almonds, to decorate

For the syrup

½ cup sugar
⅔ cup water
1 tablespoon lemon juice

1 First make the syrup, place the sugar, water and lemon juice in a smll saucepan, stir to mix and then bring to a boil and simmer for about 6–8 minutes until the syrup has thickened. Allow to cool and chill.

2 Preheat the oven to 350°F. Melt the butter in a pan. Add the sugar, flour, semolina, coconut, milk, baking powder and vanilla extract and mix thoroughly.

3 Pour the cake mixture into a shallow baking pan, flatten the top and bake in the oven for 30–35 minutes until the top is golden.

4 Remove the halva from the oven and cut into diamond-shaped lozenges. Pour the cold syrup evenly over the top and decorate with an almond placed in the center of each diamond-shaped piece.

Index